Cargo Airlines

Alan J. Wright

PLYMOUTH PRESS

Abbreviations

AOC	Air Operator's Certificate
BA	British Airways
BAC	British Aircraft Corporation
BEA	British European Airways
BOAC	British Overseas Airways Corporation
CAA	Civil Aviation Authority
Combi	Combined passenger/freight
IT	Inclusive Tour
KLM	Royal Dutch Airlines
SAS	Scandinavian Airlines System
SCD	Side Cargo Door

Acknowledgments
Grateful thanks are extended to George Pennick and Allan S. Wright for their help in compiling this book. The assistance received from a number of airlines or their representatives is also much appreciated.

First published 2000

ISBN 0 7110 2667 X (Ian Allan Publishing)
ISBN 1-882663-45-4 (Plymouth Press)

Published by Ian Allan Publishing

an imprint of Ian Allan Publishing Ltd, Terminal House, Station Approach, Shepperton, Surrey TW17 8AS.

Distributed in the United States of America by Plymouth Press Ltd, 101 Panton Road, Vergennes, VT 05491
Call: (800) 477-2398 or (802) 877-2150

Printed by Ian Allan Printing Ltd, Riverdene Business Park, Molesey Road, Hersham, Surrey KT12 4RG.

Code: 0001/82

Above: One of the former military types that was used in some numbers for freight work in the immediate postwar years was the Handley Page Halifax. *AJW*

Contents

The Development of Air Freighting

Nowadays the all-year-round availability of produce such as fruit and vegetables is taken for granted by customers, with few realising that it has only become possible following the development of the air freight industry. This cautiously began soon after the end of World War 1 when large stocks of surplus aircraft were converted for civilian use. In particular several Handley Page O/400 bombers were used to pioneer the movement of newspapers around the UK in 1919, the bundles being carried in the redundant bomb-bays. Other companies introduced domestic services to carry both passengers and freight, again mostly comprising samples of the daily press which were thought to offer the most useful and lucrative loads. Airlines also acquired some welcome income at regular intervals from the surface transport industry which frequently suffered spells of unrest. These usually resulted in a strike, so mail and similar items were therefore moved by air until an agreement was reached.

Across the Atlantic US carriers also became involved at an early stage, although most of the effort was initially concentrated on the movement of small parcels in the mid-1920s. Mail was also carried in conjunction with various rail systems throughout the 1930s, but surprisingly the airline industry did not really take a serious interest in air freight until the early 1940s. Until this point a limited amount of cargo had been carried on regular passenger schedules, but this changed on 23 December 1940 when United Air Lines inaugurated the first freight-only service in the US. Using a Douglas DC-4 for nightly flights between New York and Chicago, the enterprise was a great success, especially since it was introduced in time to assist with the heavy Christmas pressure. In due course the network was expanded as other carriers recognised the potential of air cargo, which eventually resulted in the appearance of airliners specially designed for freight operations.

In the meantime, despite many attempts few of the UK regular services were sustained in the 1920s and 1930s. This was mainly due to the lack of suitable aircraft that were capable of flying nonstop at speeds superior to those achieved by the competing railways. There was certainly no point in employing air transport if headwinds forced a refuelling stop that made progress slower than express trains. Operations were also made difficult by a distinct shortage of convenient airfields close to intended destinations, while the weather also played a significant part since there were no radio aids to assist the pilots in poor conditions.

By the mid-1930s a more positive approach was taken, resulting in the formation of Railway Air Services. This company was duly awarded a contract by the GPO for the carriage of mail over routes linking the Midlands, Northern Ireland and Scotland in conjunction with the new daily passenger services. The postal authority soon enlarged its air network, but at the same time contracted some of the work to Essex-based Hillman Airways which thereafter carried an average of some 500lb (226.8kg) of mailed items every day. However, after a modest start, the participating carriers were eventually lifting 450,000lb (204,120kg) annually by the outbreak of war in 1939. Thereafter the necessary restrictions placed on the activities of civil aircraft severely reduced the amount of freight movements by air.

Left: Although the configuration of the Argosy was designed to permit speedy loading, the type only enjoyed limited success. *AJW*

During the ensuing period the benefits of air freight became fully appreciated, with the military forces making increased use of this form of transport as the war progressed. When peace was restored in 1945 a similar situation existed to that of 25 years earlier, when a considerable number of aircraft suddenly became surplus to requirements. Numerous new airlines were launched, many by ex-RAF pilots eager to continue flying careers. Sadly few of the fledgling companies survived for very long in the difficult postwar period, although there were a few notable exceptions which went on to play a large part in the success of the present-day cargo operations.

By chance, once again it was a Handley Page product that was one of the types chosen for a new career as a civilian airliner. A military transport version of the Halifax bomber was already available as the Mk VIII, so it needed little conversion to meet the required peacetime standards. The name Halton was applied to the modified machines which entered service for both freight and passenger work with a number of operators. One of the most notable of these was London Aero & Motor Services (LAMS), formed in 1946 as a car-hire company known as Grosvenor Square Garages. The latter was already successfully operating charter flights from Elstree with a fleet of light aircraft, but the far-sighted Managing Director, Dr Graham Humby, considered that air freighting offered a far more profitable future.

Accordingly the company decided to expand its activities by purchasing six ex-RAF Halifax VIIIs for dedicated cargo work. It was not long before more examples of the type were acquired, but in the event most were used for spares. Needless to say there were many doubts raised in the industry about the viability of such an enterprise in view of the initial expenditure involved, but undaunted, the company went ahead with its scheme. With the introduction of the first member of the fleet into service, the airline adopted the LAMS title although its base remained at Elstree, hardly a suitable airfield for the use of heavy aircraft. The company was well aware of this problem and was actively searching for another site that could be developed into a flourishing freight centre. The disused USAAF base known as Station 169 located at Stansted Mountfitchet in Essex was eventually chosen, with contracts quickly agreed with the authorities in December 1946.

Despite the problems involved in the move, LAMS managed to continue its regular flights to mainland Europe. The soft fruit trade soon benefited from the daily sorties which ensured the swift movement of the tender produce from grower to customer. Nothing particularly unusual in the present day, but a noteworthy occurrence in the 1940s. However, the season was relatively short which meant alternative employment had to be found for the growing Halifax fleet at other times. A new venture was therefore devised which followed the example of the shipping industry's tramp steamers. This entailed loads being organised at various ports of call during a round-the-world-flight. There were to be no prearranged routes thereby allowing the aircraft to deviate from its course to comply with customers' wishes. The journey was completed as planned, with the much-travelled Halifax G-AIWT departing from Australia fully laden with a 14,000lb (6,350kg) load of dripping. After a six-week absence the aircraft duly arrived at Stansted, an event that officially marked the latter's opening as a civil airport. Following an inspection by the newly-installed Customs

Right: The nose-loading facility of the Bristol Freighter was very useful for loading vehicles on the car ferry services. *AJW*

Left: The CL-44 was used for a short time in the 1970s for the car ferry operations. *AJW*

department, the cargo was offloaded for its road journey to the Ministry of Food at an undisclosed destination in London.

LAMS expressed its satisfaction with the operation which, although not directly profitable, had paved the way for regular flights in the future. Strangely a second excursion along similar lines attracted no interest at all from potential customers. It was a major setback for the company and certainly hastened its demise in 1948 because with much of its activities dependent upon seasonal loads, income was insufficient to keep pace with the high operating costs incurred by the Halifaxes. In addition the airline depended too heavily upon Dr Humby for its inspiration, so when he became seriously ill his leadership skills were quickly missed. Although the company failed, it did enjoy a brief but eventful career during which it clearly demonstrated that the air freight business was indeed viable.

If there were any lingering doubts about the feasibility of air cargo, the events of 1948 finally removed them. Following the Soviet Union's action to blockade Berlin, the resulting airlift succeeded in its aim to provide the inhabitants with food and fuel for many months into 1949. While the situation was not popular with the German population, it was enthusiastically welcomed by the smaller airlines. Had LAMS survived for another few months it would have undoubtedly played its part alongside the motley collection of types and carriers engaged in the relief work. It was all very successful and was instrumental in the short-term survival of a number of financially embarrassed companies.

Many mourned the passing of the Airlift which in turn brought depression to the market with little employment in prospect for the idle fleets. Such was the scarcity of work that by 1950 all of the 41 Halifaxes participating on the German relief operation had been withdrawn. In 1952 regular cargo flights were instigated once again to overcome the problems of ferrying manufactured goods from Berlin to the Western world. Stansted-based Air Charter was the main beneficiary of this operation since the company was able to operate Avro Yorks on a regular service between the former capital and Hamburg. The airline was also responsible for the reintroduction of the postwar-built Tudor into service with the new name Super Trader in recognition of its role as a dedicated cargo carrier.

Despite the obvious advantages of air-freighting in these instances, in general the use of aircraft for such a purpose was still not standard practice by the mid-1950s. Tariffs remained high when compared with surface transport, so the industry tended to confine the use of air services to the movement of emergency loads or perishables where speed was essential. On the other hand some of the extra outlay could often be justified by the savings achieved in packaging, storage and insurance. There was also the question of suitable equipment since most of the aircraft employed were former passenger airliners. By the end of the decade the introduction of turboprops and jets resulted in the conversion of the redundant piston-engined machines which would probably have otherwise been reduced to scrap. However the real change came in 1961 when Trans Canada began operating Douglas DC-8F services across the Atlantic with the aircraft configured with a mixed passenger/freight interior. A few months later Pan American decided that the time had arrived for the introduction of the freighter version of the Boeing 707, thereby becoming the first airline to fly scheduled jet cargo services. Initially the carrier provided six transatlantic flights per week, with another three crossing the Pacific. Timings were arranged so that the European sorties made a transit stop at Shannon to allow freight destined for Paris and Rome to be transferred to one of the company's DC-7s for the onward journey while the jet visited Heathrow and Frankfurt.

Both the airline and manufacturer co-operated in the development of cargo handling devices which resulted in the use of roller tracks for the movement of the pallets inside the aircraft. They were raised from ground level by a hydraulic scissors-lift, another new piece of equipment later to become a familiar sight at all freight terminals. The 707 could accommodate a maximum of 13 pallets in its cabin, producing a payload of 80,000lb (36,290kg) over a distance of 3,300 miles (5,310km). Transit stops were programmed to take about 45min since it was not anticipated that full loads would be carried until the services were fully established.

With the availability of the DC-8 and Boeing 707, airlines now had suitable aircraft for the economic development of air cargo operations. The introduction of jets soon became a significant feature of the air freight scene, mainly because many carriers found themselves with more capacity than needed for passenger work, so alternatives were sought in order to achieve adequate utilisation. In addition, several specialist types that had been designed as freighters from the outset began to appear.

One such newcomer originated with Canadair which produced 27 examples of its Rolls-Royce Tyne-powered CL-44D for the civil market. Based on the Bristol Britannia, the most obvious difference was its swing-tail arrangement intended to facilitate rapid loading. At the time it was a revolutionary idea and allowed large items of cargo to be transferred directly from trucks into the large hold.

While operators now had a choice of several long-range types, there was still a need for a modern short/medium-range aircraft to act as a feeder. The turboprop Armstrong Whitworth (later Hawker Siddeley) Argosy filled this requirement, having been developed in the late 1950s with service entry in 1961. Its twin-boom layout allowed opening doors to be installed at both ends of the fuselage pod, which combined with the low floor level, greatly assisted the freight handling procedures. Sensibly, the cabin dimensions were chosen to enable it to accommodate the same sized pallets as those used by the mainline carriers. This compatibility was found useful in practice, yet the number of orders for the aircraft remained disappointingly small.

The rugged Bristol Freighter on the other hand was one of the early postwar products designed for general duties. It was particularly successful when used for vehicle ferry work with Silver City, Channel Air Bridge and later British Air Ferries, although its limited capacity later proved a handicap as the popularity of the cross-Channel services increased in the late 1950s. Although thoughts turned briefly to a completely new design, the Freighter's successor was an ingenious conversion of the elderly Douglas DC-4 passenger airliner. Designed and built by Southend-based Aviation Traders, the main modification involved the addition of a bulbous nose complete with opening door. There was also a small passenger cabin at the rear of the fuselage which could carry up to five vehicles on the airline's frequent services. Known as the Carvair (Car-via-Air), the type enjoyed a number of very successful and profitable years, but sadly towards the end of the 1960s this element of the air freight business began to decline due to the introduction of the

Left: The Canadair CL-44 offered a swingtail for ease of loading.
HeavyLift

modern surface ferries. So in the early 1970s the remaining car ferry operations were withdrawn, leaving the surviving Carvairs to be scrapped or sold abroad.

By this time the wide-bodied passenger airliners had entered service in some numbers, each with the ability to carry a considerable amount of freight in underfloor holds. This tended to reduce the number of all-freight aircraft required, because by using the normal scheduled passenger flights, costs could be kept at a level that specialist carriers found very difficult to match. In order to cope with the steady increase of such traffic, many airports built dedicated terminals for freight handling, with facilities provided for the receipt and dispatch of consignments using the road network. Shippers soon came to appreciate the substantial advantages to be gained by sending goods by air, a mode of transport that was no longer reserved for tender-skinned fruit and other perishables.

Of course, not all freight will conveniently fit into a container or pallet. Outsized loads require outsized aircraft, a need identified by a UK company towards the end of the 1970s. Formed as Transmeridian Air Cargo, the carrier was initially equipped with CL-44s, but later proposed to employ the former RAF Short Belfast for specialist charter work since it possessed an unobstructed hold some 90ft (27.5m) in length. Nevertheless, before the authorities were prepared to issue a type certificate, numerous modifications were specified which consumed thousands of man-hours in design and engineering, not to mention the cost of more than £3 million to the company. Subsequently known as HeavyLift, the company's business involves volumetric rather than excessively heavy loads, with two of the original five converted Belfasts still in service for this type of employment alongside the enormous Antonov An-124s operated in association with the Russian carrier Volga-Dnepr.

At an early stage in the career of Airbus Industrie it was necessary to ferry the various completed sections from the subcontractors' plants to the main assembly centre at Toulouse. An airlift proved to be the answer, so the company introduced the Super Guppy for routine delivery flights around Europe. Based on the Boeing Stratocruiser, four examples were employed for many years but in the early 1990s a replacement was needed to take over the duties from the elderly piston-engined transports. This resulted in the remarkable A300-608ST Beluga, a machine designed and built by Airbus primarily to transport newly-built airliner components. However, an increasing amount of flying for third party customers is also undertaken. This enormous machine utilises the lower fuselage, wings and powerplant of the standard airliner, but with the addition of a vast upper-deck cargo hold. The same concept is under consideration for the larger A330 and A340 series which will probably feature an even larger freight compartment.

Airbus Industrie is also in the process of developing a freight version of the proposed A3XX ultra-high-capacity passenger airliner in response to a demand from potential customers. Originally the consortium expected the cargo version to become the first derivative to be introduced some two years after the 550-seat airliner, but pressure from the market could expedite the design. Provisional figures indicate that the freighter would carry an increased payload of 150 tonnes over a distance of 6,550 miles (10,545km), figures that will require significant structural strengthening.

Nonetheless, one of the fastest growing elements of the air cargo industry has been the overnight package market which now extends worldwide. Somewhat surprisingly the first experimental air express package hub system was launched by the Indian Government in 1949. It was a novel method that was designed to speed up mail and package services between the four largest cities in India, namely Bombay, Calcutta, Delhi and Madras. Four Douglas DC-3s were employed for the scheme, each of them leaving one of the cities bound for Nagpoor, located in the centre of the country. Here the loads were systematically sorted and flown to their respective destinations via one of the hubs. Although successful, the operation was not developed by the authorities so this pioneering venture was terminated in 1951.

Another 20 years or so passed before a similar scheme was introduced in the US, a country where the vast distances involved could readily justify such an enterprise. This view was shared by a student, Frederick W. Smith, who conceived the idea while attending Yale University. In his view there were large profits to be won by a well organised operation, while the business opportunities appeared limitless. He therefore decided to form a company named

Right: The Boeing Stratocruiser provided the basis for the Super Guppy used by Airbus Industrie to ferry large sections of airliners to the Toulouse assembly plant. *AJW*

Federal Express, with the intention of using modified Dassault Falcon 20s for the nightly movements. It was an immediate success and led to rapid growth in aircraft size and fleet numbers. It was not long before other companies began to realise the potential and joined the small package industry. After FedEx came Purolator Courier in September 1976, Emery two years later in September 1978, while United Parcel Service joined the other participants in September 1982. Both DHL and Airborne Express added more competition with even the US Postal Service seeking to share some of the success by offering an overnight mail service that was achieved by flying it on scheduled airlines, usually one of the American Eagle companies.

There is little doubt that the movement of cargo by air is now an accepted part of modern living, yet to some extent it has spoilt the eager anticipation of the seasons when the various fruits and vegetables were available for a short time each year. Inevitably the market will continue to grow to meet the demand for exotic produce from faraway places, electronic goods from the Far East or an urgently-needed item in an envelope.

While this boom is welcomed by the industry, it has brought some problems in its wake. Congestion in the sky during daylight hours has long been recognised, but with the great increase in freight movements, the same hazard is becoming more serious during the night. Pilots are already making representations to the various governments for collision-avoidance equipment to be installed in freighters as in passenger airliners. The cargo traffic is also creating a heavy demand for pilots capable of flying the large jets around the world on the nightly distribution services. This in turn is causing a shortage of flightdeck crew for the passenger airlines which have traditionally recruited from the military. With the military cutbacks, this source cannot provide the same quantity of qualified pilots as before, so career prospects look good for the student pilots.

Below: Airbus A300-608ST Beluga F-GSTC was used to transport a space module from Italy to NASA at the Kennedy Space Center Florida in July 1998. *K. Buchanan via G. Pennick*

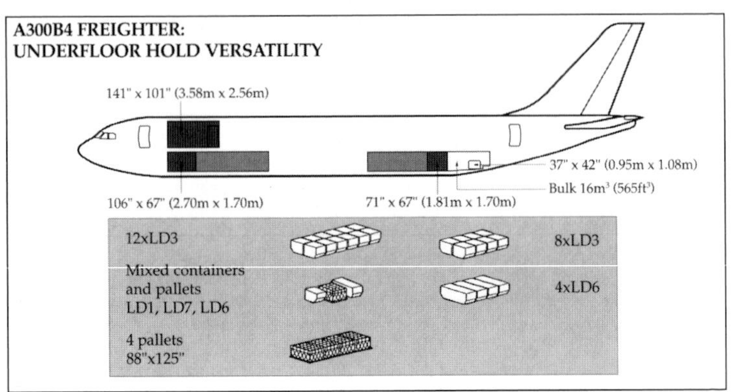

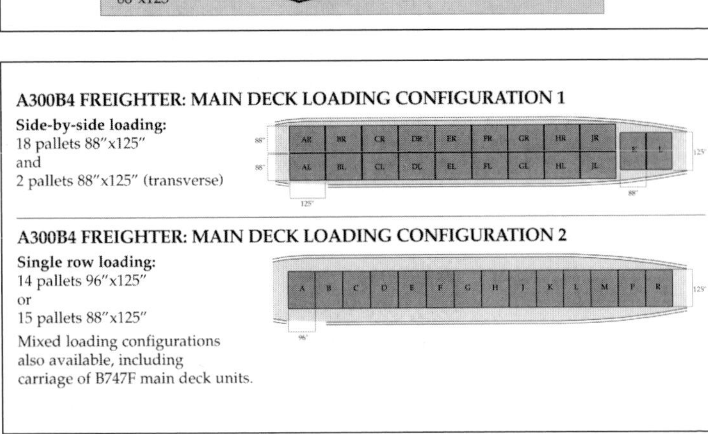

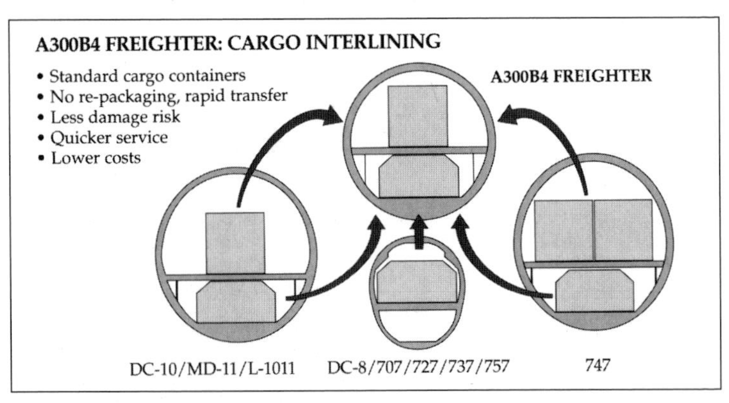

Above: A300 freighter configurations.

Live Freight

While much of the freight carried by air nowadays is containerised or securely fastened to pallets, the movement of livestock has also been offered even before World War 2. In the postwar period it was recognised that by transporting racehorses by air they arrived in good condition with a considerable saving of time. The greater the distance, the more worthwhile the airlift that offered opportunities previously thought impractical. Some of the first attempts to carry horses in the UK utilised the Miles M57 Aerovan, a small freighter which incorporated a rear opening door for ease of loading. Although an ideal arrangement, unfortunately the dimensions of the cabin restricted the size of its equine passengers to that of a pony. The Bristol Freighter overcame such handicaps and was used successfully for all forms of livestock, including racehorses. The USA can claim to have pioneered transatlantic flying by the latter in 1946, but the British independent airline Skyways became the first in the world to introduce a regular scheduled service for animals in 1957.

In the early days the creatures, ranging from elephants to bacteria, occasionally suffered harm during the course of their airborne journey due to lack of information about their needs. As a result there are now detailed regulations that are strictly applied and attract heavy penalties for infringements. Nowadays the standard of comfort and care provided has greatly improved with experience whatever the length of the journey. In fact, the accommodation could sometimes be considered superior to some intended for human passengers!

Airports for Freight

As the industry grows, so it is important that there are adequate facilities to handle the cargo efficiently, with no time lost in onward deliveries or transfers. The world's airports generally recognise this need and have constructed new terminals in many cases in order to attract even more traffic. In the past an airport measured its success in terms of passenger movements, but now there is an increasing desire to also be the largest cargo facility in terms of freight and mail handled.

As could be expected, in 1998 Memphis, Tennessee, was in the same prime position it has occupied for a number of years and is unlikely to change in the foreseeable future. This gratifying state of affairs is due almost exclusively to the presence of the world's largest air freight company, FedEx. Memphis is the carrier's headquarters and also its largest hub which receives and dispatches cargo from and to all parts of the world. In fact, almost all the freight handled is transferred from one flight to another for its onward journey. During 1998 the airport recorded nearly 2.4 million tonnes processed, an increase of 6.1% over the previous year. Los Angeles remained in second place with 1.86 million tonnes, while the runners-up were Miami (1.79 million), Hong Kong (slipped to fourth place with 1.66 million), Tokyo/Narita (1.63 million), New York/JFK (1.60 million), Frankfurt (1.46 million), Chicago O'Hare (1.44 million), Seoul (1.42 million) and Louisville, headquarters of UPS (1.39 million).

In 1997 the European top five consisted of Frankfurt, London/Heathrow, Amsterdam/Schiphol, Paris/Charles de Gaulle and Brussels. No doubt there will be some changes following the development of new hubs such as Liège in Belgium.

Cargo Airlines

ACS of Canada (CIC)

Head Office: 780 Magenta Boulevard,
Farnham, Quebec J2N 1B8, Canada
Tel: (514) 293 3656 Fax: (514) 293 5169

See ICC Air Cargo Canada

ADC Airlines (ADK)

Head Office: 84 Opebi Road, PO Box 6392,
Lagos, Nigeria
Tel: (1) 496 5750 Fax: (1) 493 3666

When the company was formed in 1991 the plan was to operate a series of passenger services with three One-Elevens. These scheduled activities within Africa duly began but by 1994 the emphasis had moved to cargo operations. At first chartered equipment was used, but in April the carrier acquired the much-travelled Boeing 707 5N-BBD. Thereafter the elderly machine has flown on the regular freight runs between Europe and Africa using Ostend as the northern terminal for its load. Later three Boeing 727s were added to the fleet in 1995, these being employed for freight work over shorter sectors.

Fleet:

Regn	*Srs*	*C/n*	*Regn*	*Srs*	*C/n*
Boeing 707			**Boeing 727**		
5N-BBD	338C	19625	5N-BBF	231F	20049
			5N-BBH	231F	2005

Above: Boeing 707 5N-BBD of ADC Airlines parked at Ostend between flights. *AJW*

Aer Turas Teoranta (ATT)

Head Office: Corballis Park, Dublin Airport, Dublin, Ireland
Tel: (1) 844 41 31 Fax: (1) 844 5049

The company started in a small way in 1962 with passenger and freight charters from its Dublin base. These were flown by one DH Rapide (EI-AML) which proved adequate for the short-haul trips that generally confined it to the UK and Eire. After two years of service it was replaced by the DC-3 EI-ANK, but during the winter of 1964/65 the company ceased flying while it reorganised itself. Activities were resumed in 1965, this time with a Douglas DC-4 carrying out all the duties, but it was not long before some expansion brought a second example into the fleet together with a pair of Bristol Freighters. These were supplemented by a number of former KLM Douglas DC-7s although not all served with Aer Turas before being sold.

The airline's first turboprop type was introduced in 1972 when an HS Argosy was leased from the Canadian company Transair. Used mainly for bloodstock movements, the aircraft did not entirely meet the Irish company's requirements and was returned to its owner.

This left a DC-4 and DC-7 to cope with the workload, but after the latter was damaged the airline announced that it had reached an agreement with Monarch Airlines for the lease-purchase of a Bristol Britannia. The machine involved had originally served with Air Charter and British United as G-ANCE, but with Aer Turas it became EI-BAA. Subsequently it served Aer Turas until 1981 when it was broken up for spares. In the meantime a second specimen had been acquired, this time from the RAF's surplus stock. Registered EI-BBH, it was used for freight charters until it was sold in 1981.

A year earlier Aer Lingus obtained a majority shareholding in the company with the result that all of the freight work was handled by the flag carrier's subsidiary. By this time a Canadair CL-44 had arrived, the first of three to serve with Aer Turas, one being the Conroy-converted Guppy variant. Also in the early 1980s the airline's first jet was delivered, this being DC-8-63F EI-BNA which had flown with both Flying Tiger and Cargolux as a freighter.

In due course another two examples of the type were taken on strength (EI-CGO and CAK), although the latter was sold in 1994. Currently Aer Turas still has the two DC-8s with which it continues its freight operations, often on behalf of other carriers. With a number of surplus TriStars available, the company acquired one to provide back-up and support to major passenger and freight airlines in 1996. This venture proved successful, resulting in two more of the breed entering service with the Irish operator. One of the trio (EI-COL) later had the distinction on 21 August 1998 of becoming the first wide-bodied type to land at Southend. The same record was not achieved by the take-off because it was decided to scrap the TriStar on site, a task completed by the end of March 1999.

Fleet:

Regn	*Srs*	*C/n*	*Regn*	*Srs*	*C/n*
Douglas DC-8			**Lockheed L-1011 TriStar**		
EI-BNA	63F	45989	EI-CNN	1	1024
EI-CGO	63F	45924			

Affretair (ZM/AFM)

Head Office: PO Box 635, Harare International Airport, Harare, Zimbabwe
Tel: (4) 57 50 09 Fax: (4) 57 50 10

Founded in 1965 as Air Trans Africa, the company began operating services with a DH Heron and a Douglas DC-7C. The first jet type was acquired in 1972 when a DC-8-55 joined the fleet, to be followed in due course by another pair to cover the growing route network radiating from Harare. In early 1980 the airline was designated as the national cargo carrier for the newly-formed Zimbabwe, with the consequence that the company's title was changed to Affretair. The regular freight services continued to serve a variety of European and African destinations, although following a strategic partnership agreement with DHL in 1997, the equipment employed is now leased from the latter.

Fleet:
Leased as required

African Airlines International (AIK)

Head Office: Airport North Road, Jkia Nairobi, PO Box 74772, Kenya
Tel: (2) 82 4333 Fax: (2) 82 3999

Formed in 1987, it was 1990 before the airline began operations, its initial activities involving passenger charter services within Africa. With the fleet of venerable Boeing 707s having reached three, the company leased a dedicated freighter (5Y-AXG) from Continental Cargo Airlines to introduce regular cargo sorties to Europe. These began in late 1990 to continue for a couple of years or so before the aircraft was reregistered as 9G-ADM on the Ghana register. At this point the aircraft was sub-leased to RACE Cargo Airlines followed by a spell with Dairo Air Services before returning to Continental, its current operator in 1999.

Fleet:

Regn	*Srs*	*C/n*	*Regn*	*Srs*	*C/n*
Boeing 707			5Y-AXR	351B	19634
5Y-AXI	330B	18927	5Y-AXW	321B	19366
5Y-AXM	330B	18819			

Above: African International Airways operates a regular cargo service to the UK with DC-8 freighters, in this case 3D-AFR. *AJW*

African International Airways (AIN)

Head Office: PO Box 569, Suite 108, Development House, Swazi Place, Mbabane, Swaziland. European Office: The Brunel Centre, Newton Road, Crawley, West Sussex RH10 2TU
Tel: (01293) 54 47 06 Fax: (01293) 61 58 00

AIA was formed in 1985 as an all-cargo carrier flying charters between Africa and Europe, together with sub-services for scheduled airlines such as Alitalia. After operating three former United Air Lines DC-8s for some years, the carrier sold one of the trio (3D-AFX) in 1998.

Fleet:

Regn	*Srs*	*C/n*	*Regn*	*Srs*	*C/n*
Douglas DC-8			3D-AFR	54F	45802
3D-ADV	54F	46012			

Air Algérie (AH/DAH)

Head Office: 1 Place Maurice-Audin, Algiers, Algeria
Tel: (2) 64 24 28 Fax: (2) 50 72 05

The airline was created by the merger of Compagnie Générale de Transport Aérien and Compagnie Air Transport in 1953. Passenger services were gradually expanded using a variety of modern types, but it was 1981 before a cargo division was set up, by which time the airline was wholly owned by the Government. Three Lockheed Hercules were acquired from the manufacturer which were used for scheduled flights to link some of the larger Algerian cities with European centres. The aircraft proved ideal for the purpose which included the movement of large and heavy items for the oil industry. In fact two are still in service with the carrier, the third being damaged beyond repair in a forced landing in 1989. Air Algérie also has a convertible Boeing 737 which is used for smaller consignments of cargo. The company lost a similar aircraft in December 1994 when it crashed on approach to Coventry where it was to pick up livestock.

Fleet:

Regn	*Srs*	*C/n*	*Regn*	*Srs*	*C/n*
Boeing 737			**Lockheed L-100 Hercules**		
7T-VES	2D6C	21287	7T-VHG	30	4880
			7T-VHL	30	4886

Air Atlanta Icelandic (CC/ABD)

Head Office: PO Box 80, IS-270 Mosfellssbaer, Iceland
Tel: 515 77 00 Fax: 515 77 66

The company was formed in February 1986 and has since established bases at Cologne, Madrid, Manchester, Jeddah and London. It specialises in the supply of additional capacity and back-up facilities for airlines requiring assistance, passenger work being its main occupation. However, it also operates two Boeing 737-200s for cargo flights between Cologne and Oslo via Copenhagen and the sector linking Cologne with Helsinki. These are flown under contract to Lufthansa. The airline's fleet also includes seven Boeing 747s, seven TriStars and a 737-300.

Fleet (Cargo):

Regn	*Srs*	*C/n*	*Regn*	*Srs*	*C/n*
Boeing 737-230			TF-ABX	230C	20257
TF-ABF	230C	20258			

Airborne Express (GB/ABX)

Head Office: 145 Hunter Drive,
Wilmington, OH 45177 USA
Tel: (513) 382 55 91 Fax: (513) 382 24 52

The history of the airline can be traced back to 1946 when Airborne Flower Traffic Association of California was founded to fly fresh flowers from Hawaii to the mainland. This activity continued for over 20 years until 1968 when the company merged with Pacific Air Freight of Seattle to create Airborne Freight Corporation with its headquarters at the northwest airport. In the meantime Elyria, Ohio-based Midwest Air Charter was operating successful courier services with small types such as Piper Aztec, Beech 18 and Learjet. With the business expanding rapidly, the company acquired five Caravelles to enable greater loads to be carried. During the following year Midwest found itself acquired by Airborne Freight which marked the launch of the present Airborne Express. The new carrier received FAA certification in April 1980, whereupon a programme of expansion was introduced. A number of NAMC YS-11 turboprops were added to the fleet to provide a fast transport for short-haul work in support of the Caravelles. There was a significant development in 1981 when Airborne purchased Clinton County AFB in Wilmington, Ohio, to become the only carrier to own and operate an airport. Within a short space of time a package sorting centre was opened to create a hub for the airline's activities, now one of the largest in the US. By the mid-1980s the ageing Caravelles had been replaced by assorted DC-9s, a type which was taken on strength in rapidly increasing numbers to become the mainstay of the carrier's fleet. It was also necessary to meet the demand for long-haul services which was accomplished by the addition of DC-8-60s. Subsequently Airborne has been responsible for a number of improvements in the air freight industry and has received a number of awards for its achievements in the process. It was inevitable that the success rate brought a degree of congestion at the Wilmington hub, so in 1995 the company laid a second runway capable of taking fully laden jets with ease. Evaluation of suitable equipment with which to eventually replace the DC-8s attracted an offer of A300 freighters from Airbus Industrie, but in the event Airborne decided on the Boeing 767-200. Negotiations resulted in the acquisition of 12 examples (later increased to 22) from All Nippon with the first pair delivered to the carrier in mid-1997. Both were then converted to freighters before entering service, a task that was undertaken by Tinco at Greensboro, US. The modifications mostly involve the installation of a strengthened floor since Airborne does not need enlarged cargo doors to be provided as its special containers fit the existing passenger doorway. Following a 15hr flight test programme, a supplemental type certificate was awarded to the airline which will receive the remainder of the former Japanese-operated 767s at intervals to the end of the decade.

Below: Airborne Express has a large fleet of DC-9s for its parcel work, N925AX being a Series 15 which started its career with Bonanza Airlines in 1965. *A. S. Wright*

Fleet:

Regn	Srs	C/n
Boeing 767		
N767AX	281PC	22785
N768AX	281PC	22786
N769AX	281PC	22787
N773AX	281PC	22788
N774AX	281PC	22789
N775AX	281PC	22790
N783AX	281PC	23016
N784AX	281PC	23017
N785AX	281PC	23018
N786AX	281PC	23019
N787AX	281PC	23020
N789AX	281PC	23021
Douglas DC-8		
N801AX	62F	46077
N802AX	62F	46134
N803AX	62F	45917
N804AX	62F	45987
N805AX	62F	45906
N808AX	62F	45954
N811AX	63F	46113
N812AX	63F	46126
N813AX	63F	46136
N814AX	63F	46041
N815AX	63F	46097
N816AX	63F	46093
N817AX	63F	45928
N818AX	63F	46075
N819AX	63F	45927
N820AX	63F	46155
N821AX	63F	46116
N822AX	63F	46079
N823AX	63F	46122
N824AX	63F	46141
N825AX	63F	46115
N826AX	63F	46061
N828AX	63F	45999
N841AX	61F	45908
N842AX	61F	46015
N843AX	61F	46017
N844AX	61F	45848
N845AX	61F	46157
N846AX	61F	46158
N847AX	61F	46031
N848AX	61F	46032
N849AX	61F	45891
N850AX	61F	45894
N851AX	61F	45940
N852AX	61F	46016

Regn	Srs	C/n
N853AX	61F	46037
Douglas DC-9		
N900AX	32	47380
N901AX	32	47381
N902AX	32	47426
N903AX	32	47427
N904AX	32	47040
N905AX	32	47147
N906AX	31	47072
N907AX	31	47203
N908AX	31	47008
N909AX	32	47148
N923AX	31	47165
N924AX	31	47403
N925AX	15	45728
N927AX	15	45717
N928AX	32	47392
N929AX	31	45874
N930AX	33	47363
N931AX	33	47384
N932AX	33	47465
N933AX	33	47291
N934AX	33	47462
N935AX	33	47413
N936AX	31	47269
N937AX	31	47074
N938AX	31	47009
N939AX	32	47201
N941AX	31	47419
N942AX	31	47552
N943AX	31	47528
N944AX	31	47550
N945AX	31	47551
N946AX	31	47003
N947AX	31	47004
N948AX	31	47065
N949AX	31	47325
N951AX	41	47616
N952AX	41	47615
N953AX	41	47608
N954AX	41	47612
N955AX	41	47619
N956AX	41	47620
N957AX	41	47759
N958AX	41	47760
N959AX	41	47761
N960AX	41	47762
N962AX	41	47768
N963AX	41	47780

Regn	Srs	C/n	Regn	Srs	C/n
N964AX	41	47781	N978AX	41	47628
N965AX	41	47498	N979AX	41	47492
N966AX	41	47510	N980AX	32	47176
N967AX	41	47509	N981AX	32	47273
N968AX	41	47499	N982AX	32	47317
N969AX	41	47464	N983AX	32	47257
N970AX	41	47494	N984AX	32	47258
N971AX	41	47497	N985AX	32	47522
N973AX	41	47511	N986AX	32	47543
N974AX	41	47623	N987AX	32	47364
N975AX	41	47512	N988AX	32	47084
N976AX	41	47596	N989AX	32	47314
N977AX	41	47513	N990AX	41	47493

Air Canada Cargo (AC/ACA)

Head Office: PO Box 14000, Montreal, Quebec H4Y 1H4, Canada
Tel: (514) 422 5000 Fax: (514) 422 7741

Trans Canada Airlines (TCA) came into being on 10 April 1937, quickly introducing express cargo flights for the movement of mail. While the country had been slow to join the world's expanding air transport industry, World War 2 played its part in accelerating the progress. The relatively young airline soon became involved in the intensive transatlantic traffic, using the civil conversion of the Lancaster for the flights to Prestwick carrying passengers, urgent mail and freight. In the postwar years the Canadair version of the DC-4 known as the North Star, together with the Constellation, took over the duties until the arrival of Douglas DC-8s in the early 1960s. The Canadian carrier became the world's first operator of the jet freighter, launching a transatlantic cargo service on 1 March 1963, one year before changing its name to Air Canada.

At this time the airline was operating the stretched DC-8 Series 60 for its long-haul passenger work, but with the arrival of the wide-bodied era in the early 1970s a start was made to convert the older machines into dedicated freighters. This process was spread over a number of years, during which time the DC-8s were also upgraded to Series 73 standard to produce considerable fuel savings for the company. The type continued to give valuable service until the mid-1990s when the last example was withdrawn for onward sale.

Nowadays Air Canada Cargo uses Boeing

Below: The Boeing 747 C-GAGA is a combi variant used by Air Canada for its cargo work. *AJW*

747 combis for its flights in addition to the freight carried by the passenger aircraft. The introduction of the Airbus A340 has greatly increased the available capacity and the type is now employed on the sectors linking Montreal-London and Paris plus Vancouver-London. The Toronto-Frankfurt operation also uses the A340, but in this case the daily visits are shared with a 747 combi. The UK capital receives two daily visits from Toronto, one operated by a Boeing 767 while the second makes use of a 747 combi. The airline's latest expansion has added a nonstop Toronto-Copenhagen schedule to its coverage, since it is anticipated that the European gateway will grow still further with the completion of the bridge between Denmark and Sweden.

Fleet:

Regn	*Srs*	*C/n*	*Regn*	*Srs*	*C/*
Boeing 747			C-GAGL	433 (SCD)	24998
C-GAGA	233B (SCD)	20977	C-GAGM	433 (SCD)	25074
C-GAGB	233B (SCD)	21627	C-GAGN	433 (SCD)	25075
C-GAGC	238B (SCD)	21354			

Air Cavrel (ACL)

Head Office: River View House, 20 Old Bridge Street, Hampton Wick, Kingston-upon-Thames, Surrey KT1 4BU
Tel: (0181) 943 99 66 Fax: (0181) 943 97 97

Formed in June 1997, Air Cavrel began operations in the following year with ad hoc freight charters from its base at Manston (Kent International) to destinations in the UK and mainland Europe. Initially one Short SD3-30 was employed for this work but this was joined by a second example as the business expanded.

Fleet:

Regn	*Srs*	*C/n*
Short SD3-30		
G-BITW	200	SH3070
G-DACS	200	SH3089

Air China Cargo (CA/CCA)

Head Office: Capital International Airport, 100621 Beijing, People's Republic of China
Tel: (10) 64 56 32 20 Fax: (10) 64 56 33 48

After the founding of the People's Republic in 1949 the Civil Aviation Administration of China (CAAC) was responsible for the operation of the country's air services until 1962. At this point it was superseded by the General Administration of Civil Aviation of China, somewhat confusingly also known as CAAC. It took over all the aviation activities in the country including the domestic network of more than 160 routes flown by the scheduled services, plus the international links with some 16 countries. Further changes were introduced in 1988 when the Government decided to split the CAAC's operating divisions into separate airlines, each with its own name. Accordingly the former Beijing-based international carrier was renamed Air China to become the largest operator in the country and now operates to some 39 cities in 28 countries.

Above: Air China's Boeing 747 B-2462 is configured as a dedicated freighter. *AJW*

Fleet (Cargo):

Regn	Srs	C/n
Boeing 747		
B-2446	2J6F (SCD)	23071
B-2448	2J6B (SCD)	23461
B-2450	2J6B (SCD)	23746
B-2456	4J6 (SCD)	24346
B-2458	4J6 (SCD)	24347
B-2460	4J6 (SCD)	24348
B-2462	2J6F (SCD)	24960

All are configured for combi working except B-2462 which is a dedicated freighter.

Regn	Srs	C/n
Lockheed L-100 Hercules		
B-3002	30	5025
B-3004	30	5027

Air Contractors (Ireland)

(AG/ABR)

Head Office: Kilronan House, Church Road, Malahide, County Dublin, Ireland
Tel: (1) 812 1900 Fax: (1) 812 1919

During the late 1990s the Hunting Group announced that it intended to dispose of its aviation interests including Hunting Cargo Airlines and its Irish associate. This was achieved in mid-1998, the purchaser being a consortium comprising the Compagnie Maritime de Belge and SAFAIR. The five Electras on strength were not included in the sale and had been out of service for some time at East Midlands. However, a separate buyer was found for all of the aircraft, although several were scrapped. Upon the completion of the company's sale in June, the new owner indicated that its name would be changed to Air Contractors (Ireland), but it would continue to operate as an independent contract carrier that included the DHL Worldwide Express obligations.

So ended a career that had started with Air Bridge Carriers in 1972 as a subsidiary of Field Aviation. Equipped with three, later four, Argosies, the company flew regular freight services to a variety of destinations, particularly the Channel Islands. During the second half of the 1970s British Airways began to phase out its Merchantman freighters, one of which was sold to Air Bridge in 1976. The type proved to be eminently suitable as a replacement for the Argosies, so BA's remaining five were acquired in 1979. Thereafter the type was used extensively for cargo charters to Europe and the Middle East, but by 1990 Air Bridge was once again considering its long-term requirements.

This time it was the Lockheed Electra that was chosen, the first example arriving at East Midlands during 1990. More of the type followed before the company announced the carrier's name had been changed to Hunting Cargo Airlines in September 1992. A smart new livery was applied to the aircraft which continued Hunting's involvement in scheduled cargo services throughout Europe. Subsequently the airline began to add Boeing 727 freighters to its fleet, although it was

October 1996 before the last ever flight was made by a Merchantman.

Hunting was one of the major cargo carriers in Europe with an expanding overnight parcels network flown for DHL Worldwide. The volume of this business was one of the reasons for becoming an early customer for the Airbus A300 freighter conversion which has a payload of 45 tonnes. During 1997 Hunting decided to consolidate all of the airline's activities in Ireland, thereby closing down the UK operation. As a result all of the British-registered aircraft received Irish identities to serve with Hunting Cargo Airlines (Ireland). This Irish link is continuing with Air Contractors.

Fleet:

Regn	*Srs*	*C/n*	*Regn*	*Srs*	*C/n*
Airbus A300B4			**Boeing 727**		
EI-EAA	203F	150	EI-HCA	225F	20382
EI-EAB	203F	199	EI-HCB	223F	19492
EI-EAC	203F	250	EI-HCC	223F	19480
EI-EAD	203F	289	EI-HCD	223F	20185
EI-EAT	203F	116	EI-HCI	223F	20183
			EI-LCH	281F	20466

Air Foyle (GS/UPA)

Head Office: Halcyon House, Luton Airport, Luton, Beds LU2 9LU
Tel: (01582) 419792 Fax: (01582)400958

Formed in 1978, Air Foyle began its career as an air taxi operator but soon commenced public transport work. The company has since been split into two divisions, Air Foyle Ltd being responsible for the cargo operations. These include TNT's nightly express parcel services that were inaugurated in May 1987 and subsequently developed until nowadays the BAe 146s link some 25 European destinations. During the day the aircraft are available for third-party charters, these often involving the movement of racehorses during the summer racing season.

Air Foyle is also able to offer transportation for the movement of outsize loads using Antonov An-124s in conjunction with the Antonov Design Bureau. This facility has been available since 1989 and also includes the operation of IL-76, An-12 and An-22 freighters worldwide. The aircraft are crewed by Antonov Design Bureau personnel and are normally based and maintained at Kiev.

A particularly important trip was made in March 1999 to meet Eutelsat's early-April launch deadline for the latest W series communications satellite project. Transported in a custom-built container, the satellite system was airlifted from Nice to the Shuttle Facility X68 at Cape Canaveral, the total weight being 68 tonnes. The flight marked the first time that one of Air Foyle/Antonov's An-124s had landed on the common landing site for all space shuttles, the runway being 15,000ft long and 300ft wide.

Fleet:

Regn	Srs	C/n	Regn	Srs	C/n
Antonov An-124			**BAe 146**		
UR-82007	100	19530501005	See under TNT		
UR-82008	100	19530501006			
UR-82009	100	19530501007	**Ilyushin Il-76**		
UR-82027	100	19530502108	UR-UCC	MD	0083484531
UR-82029	100	19530502630			

Air France Cargo (AF/AFR)

Head Office: 45 Rue de Paris, F-95747
Roissy-CDG, France
Tel: (1) 41 56 78 00 Fax: (1) 41 56 70 29

Since its creation on 30 August 1933 by the merging of an assortment of small carriers, the French national airline has always strived to remain in the forefront of the air transport industry. The airline has a cargo division operating a fleet comprising eight Boeing 747-200 dedicated freighters and 14 combi-configured variants for worldwide services, although cargo is also uplifted on passenger services dependent on space.

Fleet (Cargo)

Regn	Srs	C/n	Regn	Srs	C/n
Boeing 747			F-GCBH	228B (SCD)	23611
F-BPVR	228F (SCD)	21255	F-GCBI	228B (SCD)	23676
F-BPVS	228B (SCD)	21326	F-GCBJ	228B (SCD)	24067
F-BPVT	228B (SCD)	21429	F-GCBK	228F (SCD)	24158
F-BPVX	228B (SCD)	21731	F-GCBL	228F (SCD)	24735
F-BPVZ	228F (SCD)	21787	F-GCBM	228F (SCD)	24879
F-BTDG	2B2B (SCD)	22514	F-GETA	3B3 (SCD)	23413
F-BTDH	2B3B (SCD)	22515	F-GETB	3B3 (SCD)	23480
F-GBOX	2B3F (SCD)	21835	F-GISA	428 (SCD)	25238
F-GCBB	228B (SCD)	22272	F-GISB	428 (SCD)	25302
F-GCBD	228B (SCD)	22428	F-GISC	428 (SCD)	25599
F-GCBE	228F (SCD)	22678	F-GISD	428 (SCD)	25628
F-GCBG	228F (SCD)	22939	F-GISE	428 (SCD)	25630

The Boeing 747 freighter F-BPVR has served Air France since October 1976. *AJW*

Airfreight Express (AFX)

This new UK cargo airline was due to start operations in April 1999, but these had to be postponed until September. The company intends to provide a scheduled freight link between Heathrow, Gatwick, Manchester, Glasgow and New York/Kennedy International using a single leased Boeing 747.

Fleet:

Regn	*Srs*	*C/n*
Boeing 747		
G-GAFX	245F (SCD)	20827

Air Hong Kong (LD/AHK)

Head Office: Block 2, Tien Chu Centre, 1E Mok Cheong Street, Kowloon, Hong Kong, China
Tel: (852) 2761 8588 Fax: (852) 2761 8586

The airline was founded in November 1986 in order to provide long-haul cargo services. These began on a charter basis in February 1988, but became scheduled flights when approval was received in 1989. A large number of destinations were added to the network which were initially served by a pair of elderly Boeing 707s. It was not long before more efficient equipment was acquired as replacements, the newcomers being two Boeing 747-100s which had already been converted to full freighter status. During 1994 Hong Kong-based Cathay Pacific took a 75% stake in the airline, followed two years later by the arrival of three former Varig 747-200s to replace the older variants. The airline has used Manchester as its UK gateway for its daily Hong Kong sorties for some years.

Fleet:

Regn	*Srs*	*C/n*
Boeing 747		
B-HMD	2L5B (SCD)	22105
B-HME	2L5B (SCD)	22106
B-HMF	2L5B (SCD)	22107

Air India Cargo (AI/AIC)

Head Office: Air India Building, Nariman Point, Mumbai 400021, India
Tel: (22) 202 41 42 Fax: (22) 202 48 97

Privately-owned Tata Airlines was the forebear of Air India and flew the first load of mail from Karachi to Mumbai (Bombay) via Ahmedabad on 15 October 1932. After World War 2 Air India became the new flag carrier when it was formed in 1946, although 'International' was added to the title after the country's independence two years later. This identity was then retained until 1962 when the company reverted to its original name. During this period the airline carried out its initial cargo operations with a DC-3 in 1954, giving it the distinction of being the first Asian company to operate freighters. Air India's equipment kept pace with modern developments with the rapid traffic growth matched by the introduction of jets at an early stage. In 1971 the first wide-bodied types were delivered, although it was 1988 before two combi Boeing 747-300s began to operate to Europe from Bombay and Delhi on a five-times-weekly schedule. Although large quantities of freight can be accommodated in the main deck compartment, Air India also contracts dedicated cargo carriers such as Emery, Evergreen and Aeroflot to supply additional capacity on a long-term basis.

Fleet:

Regn	*Srs*	*C/n*
Boeing 747		
VT-EPW	337 (SCD)	24159
VT-EPX	337 (SCD)	24160
VT-ESM	437 (SCD)	27078
VT-ESN	437 (SCD)	27164
VT-ESO	437 (SCD)	27165
VT-ESP	437 (SCD)	27214
Douglas DC-8		
N791FT	73CF	46045

Air Jet (BC/AIJ)

Head Office: BP-10297, F-95700 Roissy-CDG, France
Tel: (1) 49 19 73 00 Fax: (1) 48 62 50 80

In 1980 the French Air Services Group began passenger and freight charters under the title Air Jet. The company employed a Friendship 400 for the services which included a scheduled run between

Avignon and Lyon, while overnight parcels movements were carried out from Paris to Avignon, Bordeaux and Lyon. Eventually five of the type were operated, all equipped with a large cargo door in the forward fuselage with the ability for a quick-change to passenger working with 48 seats. In 1991 the company acquired its first jet type, a BAe 146-200, also a quick-change variant, one of the first in mainland Europe. The Friendships were sold to the German carrier WDL in 1995, but during the next year Air Jet was operating three 146s. These carried on the regular overnight operations with visits to Avignon, Strasbourg and Toulouse. During the day the company operated a scheduled service between London City and Paris, but this was discontinued in mid-1997.

Fleet:

Regn	Srs	C/n	Regn	Srs	C/n
BAe 146			F-GOMA	200QC	E2211
F-GLNI	200QC	E2188			
F-GMMP	200QC	E2176			

Air Sofia (CT/SFB)

Head Office: 64 Patriarch Evtimi Boulevard, BG 1000 Sofia, Bulgaria
Tel: (2) 981 08 80 Fax: (2) 980 29 07

The company began operations in February 1992 with ad hoc freight charters to domestic and international destinations as distant as the Far East and South America. It is the largest Bulgarian independent airline and maintains a 24hr well-equipped control office to ensure up-to-the-minute information regarding planning, loading and flight organisation. In addition to its charter work, Air Sofia also wet-leases aircraft to other carriers, the fleet still consisting of the Russian-built types acquired at its original launch.

Fleet:

Regn	Srs	C/n	Regn	Srs	C/n
Antonov An-12			LZ-SFN	BP	02340806
LZ-SFA	BP	02348007	LZ-SFS	BP	6344308
LZ-SFJ	BP	4342105	**Antonov An-26**		
LZ-SFK	BP	02341901	LZ-SFH	-	3904
LZ-SFL	BP	4342101			

Air Transport International (ATN)

Head Office: 3800 Rodney Parham Road, Little Rock, Arkansas 72212, USA
Tel: (501) 224 8175 Fax: (501)225 2458

Although formed as US Airways in 1979, the company operated as Interstate Airlines to provide cargo services for the express-package industry, the Government's Department of Defence and the motor manufacturers. Much of this work was contracted by United Parcel Service (UPS), so when the latter ended its association in 1987, Interstate was obliged to seek bankruptcy protection. The company restarted in 1988 using the name Air Transport International before merging with ICX International Cargo Express in 1994, the combined force being purchased by BAX Global in 1998. Much of ATI's work is on behalf of its parent company using a large fleet of DC-8s.

Fleet:

Regn	Srs	C/n	Regn	Srs	C/n
Douglas DC-8			N41CX	62CF	46129
N21CX	62CF	45955	N61CX	62CF	46142
N31CX	62CF	45911	N728PL	62CF	45918

Regn	Srs	C/n	Regn	Srs	C/n
N786AL	63AF	46121	N829BX	71AF	45994
N820BX	71AF	46065	N830BX	71AF	45973
N821BX	71AF	45811	N861PL	61AF	45964
N822BX	71AF	45813	N867BX	63AF	46049
N823BX	71AF	46064	N868BX	63AF	46034
N824BX	71AF	45946	N869BX	63AF	46035
N825BX	71AF	45978	N870BX	63AF	46036
N826BX	71AF	45998	N906R	63AF	46087
N827BX	71AF	45971	N8969U	62AF	46070
N828BX	71AF	45993	N8974U	62AF	46110

Alitalia Cargo (AZ/AZA)

Head Office: Centro Direzionale, Viale Alessandro Marchetti III, I-00148 Rome, Italy
Tel: (6) 6562 2020 Fax: (6) 6562 4733

After World War 2 a number of airlines were started in Italy, several expressing an interest in the introduction of domestic scheduled services. It was not long before financial considerations brought a series of mergers until only Aerolinee Italiane Internazionali (Alitalia) and Linee Aeree Italiane (LAI) remained active. Both companies gradually developed their scheduled operations and began adding international routes to the expanding networks as modern equipment replaced the immediate postwar types. However, by 1957 the Government realised it seemed somewhat uneconomic to have two major carriers serving the same market. Therefore on 1 September 1957 the affairs of LAI were formally taken over by Alitalia. Cargo services were flown with two converted DC-7s in the late 1950s, but with the introduction of DC-8s in the next decade, this type replaced the piston-engined machines for the long-haul freight trips. From the early 1970s Boeing 747s began to join the fleet, several being combi configured or in the guise of dedicated freighters. The latter were employed on the Far East routes, although the aircraft also visited New York on a regular basis. In many cases the Rome-originating sorties used Milan (Malpensa) as a transit stop for both west and eastbound flights due to the considerable volume of traffic generated by the region around the northern Italian city.

In 1991 Alitalia began to take delivery of eight MD-11s intended mainly for the Far East and South American sectors. Five of the aircraft were designed for combi working, with a capability of carrying 204 passengers in the front cabin, together with six pallets in the rear compartment. Unlike the freight-only version which has a forward loading door, the combi version is equipped with a similar entrance towards the rear of the fuselage, both being on the port side.

Alitalia Cargo now covers a vast network to serve more than 400 destinations throughout five continents, made possible by a series of co-operation agreements with other airlines. The high standards and reliability of the services are recognised by the customers and result in the Italian flag carrier transporting items as varied as Formula One cars, valuable works of art, high-tech products, perishable goods and flowers. The company has also set up a subsidiary road feeder organisation which provides an efficient support service.

Fleet (Cargo):

Regn	Srs	C/n	Regn	Srs	C/n
Boeing 747			**McD Douglas MD-11**		
I-DEMC	243B (SCD)	22506	I-DUPA	C	48426
I-DEMF	243B (SCD)	22508	I-DUPE	C	48427
I-DEMR	243F (SCD)	22545	I-DUPI	C	48428
			I-DUPO	C	48429

Amerijet International (JH/AJT)

Head Office: 498 South West 34th Street, Fort Lauderdale, Florida 33315, USA
Tel: (954) 359 0077 Fax: (954) 359 7899

The airline was formed in 1974 to join the small package and express delivery industry. After starting operations with one leased Learjet, the company had added more of the type by the early 1980s. The first of three Boeing 727s joined the fleet in 1985 whereupon Amerijet became a freight-only carrier flying under contract to Purolator Courier (merged with Emery in 1987), Airborne Express, DHL, FedEx and UPS. More B727s were subsequently acquired including six former Pan Am specimens long withdrawn by the carrier. Nowadays the airline provides scheduled cargo services to 16 destinations in North and South America and Mexico, together with another 21 Caribbean locations, some on behalf of DHL and BAX Global.

Fleet (Cargo):

Regn	*Srs*	*C/n*	*Regn*	*Srs*	*C/n*
Boeing 727			N598AJ	212F	21947
N196AJ	227F	20838	N794AJ	227F	21243
N296AJ	251F	21156	N797AJ	2X3F	22609
N395AJ	233F	21100	N895AJ	224F	20660
N397AJ	2X3F	22608	N994AJ	233F	20942
N495AJ	233F	20937	N83428	2F9F	21426

Arrow Air (JW/APW)

Head Office: Miami International Airport, PO Box 026062, Miami, FL 22102 USA
Tel: (305) 526 09 00 Fax: (305) 526 09 33

The company was founded in 1947 by George E. Batchelor, the Chairman of the US supplemental carrier Capitol International Airways. In those days known as Arrow Airways, the carrier established its base at Torrance Municipal Airport, Lomita, California, from where it operated Douglas DC-3s on passenger and cargo services within the State. This activity continued until 1954 at which point flying was suspended.

Eventually the airline was reactivated by its founder in 1980, adopting the revised title of Arrow Air for the company. Initially the effort was concentrated on cargo flights, but after a year or so the business was expanded to include passenger charters from Miami to points in the Caribbean, South America and Europe. The carrier was also contracted by Western Airlines to operate its scheduled Denver-London/Gatwick route in 1981, but the service was dropped in 1982 due to a shortage of passengers.

Although Arrow Air began by assembling a collection of assorted Boeing 707 convertibles, numerous DC-8 variants were also acquired for both passenger and freight work. However, the airline experienced some turbulent times in the mid-1980s, mainly due to the crash of a DC-8-63 at Gander. As a result of this disaster the carrier was grounded by the US FAA in February 1986 which coincided with Arrow seeking the protection under Chapter 11 of the Federal bankruptcy code. In due course the company emerged from this difficult period, but when restarting it dropped its passenger work to concentrate on freight charters. These were flown worldwide, but in addition a number of scheduled links were operated between Miami, New York, San Juan and Haiti. In 1993 Arrow resumed passenger services once again, this time with Boeing 727s, but subsequently the fleet reverted to all-freight work with DC-8s and converted TriStar 200s. A major change came in February 1999 when it was announced that Fine Air Services had agreed to acquire the stock and operating assets of the airline, although it was expected that Arrow Air would retain its identity.

Currently Arrow flies over 90 weekly scheduled round trips and is one of the largest carriers of international air cargo at Miami. This is achieved with the help of the DC-8-62s which can carry 14 pallets with a payload of 95,000lb (43,000kg), the Srs 63 with 18 pallets and a payload of 110,000lb (49,900kg), while the wide-bodied TriStar has a capacity for 26 pallets and a payload of 126,000lb (57,000kg).

Fleet (Cargo):

Regn	*Srs*	*C/n*	*Regn*	*Srs*	*C/n*
Douglas DC-8			**Lockheed L-1011 TriStar**		
N441J	63F	45988	N306GB	200F	1138
N661AV	63F	45969	N307GB	200F	1131
N791AL	62F	46150	N308GB	200F	1133
N1803	62F	45895			
N1804	62F	45896			

Asiana Airlines (OZ/AAR)

Head Office: PO Box 142, Asiana Building, 10-1, 2-Ka Hoehyun-Dong, Chubg-Ku, Seoul 100052, South Korea
Tel: (2) 758 81 14 Fax: (2) 758 80 08

The airline was formed by the Kumho Group in 1988 in accordance with the South Korean Government's policy to establish a second flag carrier. Although at the outset operations were confined to domestic passenger services, it was not long before international destinations were added to the network, the first of the additional routes linking Japanese cities with Seoul. Although the carrier's first Boeing 747-400 was delivered in 1992, it was December 1994 before a freighter variant joined the company. Asiana began a twice-weekly London service on 9 November 1998, routing via Tashkent and Amsterdam to Stansted on Wednesday and Sunday. The airline provides a local road feeder service with bonded transportation between the main London airports.

Fleet (Cargo):

Regn	*Srs*	*C/n*	*Regn*	*Srs*	*C/n*
Boeing 747			**Boeing 767**		
HL-7419	48EF (SCD)	25781	HL-7506	38EFER	25760
HL-7420	48EF (SCD)	25783	HL-7507	38EFER	25761
HL-7422	48EF (SCD)	28367	HL-7528	38EFER	29129
HL-7424	48EF (SCD)	28551			
HL-7426	48EF (SCD)	27603			
HL-	48EF (SCD)	-			

Below: Asiana now operates regular cargo services into Stansted using Boeing 747-400s such as HL-7422. *AJW*

Atlantic Airlines (AAG)

Head Office: Hangar 5, Coventry Airport, Baginton, Coventry, West Midlands CV8 3AZ
Tel: (1) 203 30 75 66 Fax: (1) 203 30 77 03

Originally formed as General Aviation Services, the Jersey-based company became an air-taxi operator in September 1969. The business was expanded in 1977 when a number of Douglas DC-3s were obtained for both freight and passenger charters, at the same time adopting the new title of Air Atlantique. The aircraft were subsequently employed on a wide variety of contract and ad hoc work throughout Europe, but In 1983 the freight division became known as Atlantic Air Transport with its base established at Stansted. At that time it was a quiet spot with no problems concerning slots and congestion, although road access was poor.
By 1986 it was apparent that all would change when it was confirmed that the Essex airport was to be developed. Since its premises were to disappear in the interest of progress, it was decided to transfer the company to Coventry where its new corporate headquarters and maintenance base were established. Soon after this event a pair of DC-6s were added to the fleet to undertake the longer-range flights, leaving the DC-3s to continue the ad hoc cargo work together with night mail operations and marine pollution control. A growing need for a larger capacity type became evident in the mid-1990s which resulted in the introduction of several Lockheed Electras. These immediately began to play a part in the overnight parcels industry under contract to DHL, while car manufacturers also became regular customers for carrying urgently needed components between plants. More reorganisation in early 1998 resulted in the creation of Atlantic Airlines, the new name combining the cargo and passenger operations of the Air Atlantique Group of companies.

Above: Atlantic Airlines has two DC-6s in service, one of which is G-SIXC. *AJW*

Below: Electra G-LOFD is one of a growing number flown by Atlantic Airlines. *AJW*

Fleet (Cargo):

Regn	Srs	C/n
Douglas DC-3		
G-AMPZ	C-47B	32872
G-AMRA	C-47B	26735
(G-AMCA, G-AMHJ, G-AMPO, G-AMPY, G-AMSV, G-AMYJ and G-ANAF modified for pollution control on behalf of Department of Transport or stored)		
Douglas DC-6A		
G-APSA	-	45497
G-SIXC	-	45550
Lockheed L-188 Electra		
G-FIJR	L188PF	1138
G-FIJV	L188AF	1129
G-FIZU	L188CF	2014
G-LOFB	L188CF	1131
G-LOFC	L188CF	1100
G-LOFD	L188CF	1143
G-LOFE	L188CF	1144

Atlas Air (5Y/GTI)

Head Office: 538 Commons Drive, Golden, CO 80401, USA
Tel: (303) 526 50 50 Fax: (303) 526 50 51

In 1992 it was apparent that the air freight industry was growing rapidly and that there was a distinct danger that there would be insufficient capacity to cope with the demand. Atlas Holdings therefore formed a new carrier known as Atlas Air which was intended to offer long-haul cargo equipment to major airlines in need. The company set about the task of building up a fleet of dedicated Boeing 747 freighters by converting available Srs 200s, a variant that could lift and carry an impressive load over long distances. The company successfully located aircraft suitable for the programme, the sources being mainly Lufthansa, Thai International, Cargolux and Alitalia.

As a result, by the end of 1998 the company operated the world's largest fleet of 747-200 freighters, a fact that has helped it to also become the third largest cargo airline in the world (in terms of freight carried) behind only FedEx and UPS. During the year the airline acquired another four used 747-200Fs which received thorough overhauls before joining customers' fleets. Additionally, Atlas ordered 10 747-400s for delivery between 1998 and 2001, five of which had been delivered by early 1999, whereupon two were placed with both FedEx and Cargolux. The fifth example (N495MC) was painted in full British Airways World Cargo livery before leaving the manufacturer since it has been allocated to a new service between Hong Kong and London to be operated on the flag carrier's behalf by Atlas Air. It is just one of the routes to 76 cities in 42 countries that Atlas Air's aircraft visit on a regular basis. Frequent users of the US operator's services include Alitalia, British Airways, Cargolux, China Airlines, Emirates, El Al, Fast Air, FedEx, Iberia, SAS and Thai Airways International.

Fleet (Cargo):

Regn	Srs	C/n
Boeing 747		
N408MC	47UF (SCD)	29261
N409MC	47UF (SCD)	-
N412MC	47UF (SCD)	-
N491MC	47UF (SCD)	29252
N492MC	47UF (SCD)	29253
N493MC	47UF (SCD)	29254
N494MC	47UF (SCD)	29255
N495MC	47UF (SCD)	29256
(BA livery)		
N496MC	47UF (SCD)	29257
N497MC	47UF (SCD)	29258
N498MC	47UF (SCD)	29259
N499MC	47UF (SCD)	29260
N505MC	2D3BF (SCD)	21251
N506MC	2D3BF (SCD)	21252
N507MC	230BF (SCD)	21380
N508MC	230BF (SCD)	21644
N509MC	230BF (SCD)	21221
N512MC	230BF (SCD)	21220

Above: Atlas Air has an impressive collection of Boeing 747 freighters, of which N808MC is an example. *K. Buchanan via G. Pennick*

Regn	Srs	C/n	Regn	Srs	C/n
N516MC	243BF (SCD)	22507	N534MC	2F6BF (SCD)	21832
N517MC	243BF (SCD)	23300	N535MC	2F6BF (SCD)	21833
N518MC	243BF (SCD)	23476	N536MC	228F (SCD)	21576
N522MC	2D7BF (SCD)	21783	N537MC	271C (SCD)	22403
N523MC	2D7BF (SCD)	21782	N538MC	271C (SCD)	21964
N524MC	2D7BF (SCD)	21784	N539MC	271C (SCD)	21965
N526MC	2D7BF(SCD)	22337	N808MC	212BF (SCD)	21048
N527MC	2D7BF (SCD)	22471	N809MC	228F (SCD)	20887
N528MC	2D7BF (SCD)	22472	N	243B (SCD)	22512

BAC Express (RPX)

Head Office: BAC House, Bonehurst Road, Horley, Surrey RH6 8QG
Tel: (01293) 821621 Fax: (01293) 821204

Since operations started in September 1994, BAC Express has successfully acquired a number of contracts from the Royal Mail, Parcel Force and major courier companies to add to its existing ad hoc cargo activities. The airline employs both Fokker F-27s and Short SD3-60s for the work, the Dutch-built type being capable of carrying 6 tonnes of freight, roughly double that of the 360. However, the latter can be rapidly converted for passenger flying when required, a useful facility during the summer season when BAC uses the type for regular charters to the Channel Islands from a number of UK regional airports. The company also undertakes an increasing amount of sub-contract work for airlines short of capacity, with aircraft out-stationed at Belfast, Cardiff, Edinburgh, Exeter, Isle of Man and Southend for quick response.

Fleet (Cargo):

Regn	Srs	C/n	Regn	Srs	C/n
Fokker F-27			G-CLAS	100	SH3635
G-BVOB	500	10366	G-EXPS	100	SH3661
G-BVOM	500	10381	G-ISLE	200	SH3638
G-BVZW	500	10425	G-KBAC	300	SH3758
G-JEAD	500	10627	G-LEGS	200	SH3637
			G-OBOH	200	SH3713
Short SD3-60			G-OCEA	300	SH3762
G-CBAC	100	SH3675	G-OJSY	100	SH3603
G-CEAL	300	SH3761			

BAX Global (8W)

Head Office: 16808 Armstrong Avenue, PO Box 19571, Irvine, CA 92623, USA
Tel: (419) 867 9911 Fax: (419) 867 0138

When formed on 15 June 1972, the company was known as Burlington Northern Air Freight, serving 10 cities spread around the US. Within five years of its inception, the airline became one of the country's top 10 international freight forwarders with a total of 61 offices and 820 employees. During 1980 Burlington Air Express was added, thereby offering small package overnight express services. Two years later the organisation became a part of the Pittston Co which at the time was the largest acquisition in air freight history. Soon after this transaction, in 1985 the company decided to assemble its own fleet, whereupon 13 machines consisting of Boeing 707, 727 and Douglas DC-8s began to fly from the first temporary hub in Fort Wayne, Indiana. Unusually at the time, the operation of all the aircraft was contracted out and flown on behalf of Burlington in the latter's full livery by Buffalo Airways, Deverian Airways, Orion Air, Rosenbalm Aviation, Southern Air Transport and Spirit of America Airlines. Barely a year later the company considered that its name needed to reflect its business, so Burlington Northern Air Freight changed its name and logo to Burlington Air Express Inc.
During the early 1990s the carrier moved into its newly-constructed hub at Toledo, Ohio. This custom-built facility is capable of processing four million pounds (1,814,000kg) of freight per night, ranging from small packages weighing 10lb (4.5kg) to shipments of virtually any size that often weigh thousands of pounds.

When Burlington Air Express celebrated its 25th anniversary in 1997, its career had developed to the point where it could offer overnight and second-day delivery to every major North American business community, together with the movement of air freight worldwide. It was to recognise this capability that the company decided to change its name to BAX Global, which is now one of the world's leading international freight transportation companies.

Fleet (Cargo):

Regn	*Srs*	*C/n*
Boeing 727		
N858AA	223F	21085
N6806	223F	19481
N6807	223F	19482
N6831	223F	20184
Douglas DC-8		
N799AL	62F	45922
N820BX	71F	46065
N821BX	71F	45811
N822BX	71F	45813
N823BX	71F	46064
46064N824BX	71F	45946
N825BX	71F	45978
N826BX	71F	45998
N827BX	71F	45971
N828BX	71F	45993
N829BX	71F	45994
N830BX	71F	45973
N861PL	61F	45964
N867BX	63CF	46049
N868BX	63F	46034
N869BX	63F	46035
N870BX	63F	46036

British Airways World Cargo (BA/BAW)

Head Office: PO Box 10, Speedbird House, London Heathrow Airport, Hounslow, Middlesex TW6 2JA
Tel: (0181) 759 5511 Fax: (0181) 562 9930

Although British Airways is one of the top five international cargo carriers, it no longer has its own freight-only aircraft in the fleet to operate the services. The last such machine on strength was the Boeing 747-236F G-KILO which was sold in 1982 to join Cathay Pacific. Since that time BA World Cargo has had an agreement to take all of the available capacity from BA's passenger aircraft, an arrangement that has proved highly successful. Nevertheless, in early 1999 the company acquired a dedicated freighter once again, albeit a Boeing 747-400F on wet-lease from the US specialist Atlas Air. World Cargo also uses chartered machines for the three-times-weekly Hong Kong sorties, a weekly flight from Johannesburg, a one-way service from Nairobi and a twice-weekly link with Tel Aviv using a wet-leased Channel Express A300. In order to maintain its growth, World Cargo has expanded its operations to make greater use of the other London airports, with all out-sourced freighter movements being transferred from Gatwick to Stansted.

For many years cargo handling at Heathrow has been carried out in accommodation built in the 1960s and completely unsuited to the enormous growth. However, in early May 1999 this all changed when World Cargo officially opened its new spacious Cargocentre on the south side of the airport. Capable of handling up to one million tonnes of freight annually, the premises are equipped with every modern device including refrigeration units for a wide variety of perishable goods destined for supermarket shelves. It is essential that the onward transport is available without delay, so World Cargo's trucking system is operated in a similar manner to the airborne section of the journey. The work is contracted to companies that employ trailers equipped with roller beds, since ease of handling the containers is the key to faster turn-rounds when undoubtedly time is of the essence.

Fleet (Cargo):

Regn	*Srs*	*C/n*	
Boeing 747			(leased from Atlas Air)
N495MC	47UF	29256	

Capacity purchased as necessary from BA mainline fleet.

British World Airlines (VF/BWL)

Head Office: Viscount House, Southend Airport, Essex SS2 6YL
Tel: (01702) 354435 Fax: (01702) 331914

Throughout its more than 50 years career, the airline has always been involved in the movement of freight. This includes the successful car ferry operations in the 1950s and 1960s and the later contract work for the Post Office and courier companies. Since the retirement of the Viscounts, BWA has developed its sub-service work for other airlines offering both the One-Eleven and the BAe ATP as back-up equipment. The first of the latter type was delivered in September 1997 and by January 1999 had been joined by three more of the breed. Eventually the airline envisages that its ATP fleet will increase to 10, such is the potential market for the 68-seat aircraft. All are configured for Quick-Change duties and are capable of lifting 6.5 tonnes of freight when required for ad hoc or contract cargo charters.

Left: Most of the Viscounts that were used for mail and parcel work retained the normal passenger doors for loading purposes, but one or two were modified with a much larger opening in the forward fuselage. *British World*

Right: The Viscount Freighter could handle large items of freight. *British World*

Fleet (Cargo):

Regn	*Srs*	*C/n*	*Regn*	*Srs*	*C/n*
BAe One-Eleven			**BAe ATP**		
G-OBWA	518FG	232	G-OBWL	-	2057
G-OBWB	518FG	202	G-OBWM	-	2058
G-OBWD	518FG	203	G-OBWN	-	2059
G-OBWE	531FS	242	G-OBWO	-	2060

A pair of ATR-72s are also operated under contract to Shell, although one (G-OILB) is on a long lease to CityFlyer Express as G-BYTP.

Capital Cargo International Airlines (PT/CCI)

Head Office: 6200 Hazeltine National Drive, Orlando, FL32822, USA
Tel: (407) 855 2004 Fax: (407) 855 6620

The airline began operations in 1996 having received its certificate from the FAA. Its role is mainly to provide capacity to domestic and foreign carriers which prefer to utilise these services instead of expanding their own fleets for short periods. Capital can also provide the necessary transport for freight companies that have a short-term need for an aircraft yet do not wish to enter the air transport business. Such contracts generally require the airline to supply the machine, crew, maintenance and insurance, leaving the customer to meet all other expenses including fuel. As an added facility, the carrier is able to supply cargo warehousing through its wholly-owned subsidiary Capital Cargo Logistics. Currently the Orlando-based airline operates the high gross weight version of the Boeing 727 which meets the Stage II or III noise regulations.

Fleet (Cargo):

Regn	*Srs*	*C/n*	*Regn*	*Srs*	*C/n*
Boeing 727			N898AA	223F	22014
N128NA	2J7F	20879	N899AA	223F	22015
N227JL	214F	20875	N1279E	2Q6F	21971
N308AS	227F	22002			
N357KP	230F	20675			

Cargo Air Lines (ICL)

Head Office: 11 Galgale Haplada Street, 46722, Israel
Tel: (9) 952 6666 Fax: (9) 951 3232

Although the Israeli carrier Cargo Air Lines was established in 1977, it was in fact an agency that arranged for cargo capacity to be leased from El Al. In the spring of 1999 the company received the necessary scheduled service licences and approval for it to begin independent freight services. Needless to say, this development produced objections from the national carrier, but the Government decreed that the cargo market should be open to competition. Unlike El Al, CAL will be able to operate on the Jewish Sabbath, which naturally raised more protests. Start-up for the new services was aimed at the end of 1999, using Liège in Belgium as the main European hub with Amsterdam also included in its network. Much of the business in the past has included the movement of perishable produce from Israel and this is set to continue.

Fleet (Cargo):

Regn	*Srs*	*C/n*	*Regn*	*Srs*	*C/n*
Boeing 747			4X-AXL	245F (SCD)	22150
4X-AXK	245F (SCD)	22151			

Cargo Lion (TLX)

Head Office: Lion Aviation Building, Findel Airport, Luxembourg, L-1110 Luxembourg
Tel: (352) 422 58 51 Fax: 9352) 422 58 52 22

During the summer of 1991 the idea of launching a new freight airline was conceived, but with the intended title of Swisscargo being unavailable, the name Cargo Lion was adopted by the founders. This was chosen in honour of Flying Tigers, an airline for which there was much respect in the industry. The next step involved acquiring a suitable type for the duties envisaged, but it was soon found that due to the restrictive regulations applied by the Swiss authorities, it was no longer possible to register either a DC-8 or a Boeing 707 in the country for age reasons.

While it constituted a major setback, there was a solution to the problem by forming the airline elsewhere in Europe. By chance the French carrier Minerve was selling its DC-8-62F F-GDJM at the time, so it was not long before Cargo Lion became the new owner. While it was undergoing maintenance checks, arrangements were made to set up an operating base at Ostend, an airport much used by the air cargo industry. The DC-8 was duly delivered on 30 July 1992, with the first commercial sortie taking place two days later with a return trip between Ostend and Accra on behalf of Race Air Cargo.

After a period of consolidation Cargo

Below: Douglas DC-8-62F LX-TLA is one of three operated by Cargo Lion. *G. Pennick*

Lion began to gain some long-term contracts with the major airlines, at the same time gradually reducing the amount of ad hoc flying undertaken. Such was the demand for its services, that by late 1993 it was evident that some expansion was rapidly becoming necessary. Talks began for the possible purchase of Aer Turas, but in the event its Aer Lingus parent chose a management buy-out of the company. There was greater success in 1994 when it was decided to acquire Translux International Airlines, a newcomer being formed in Luxembourg. With this transaction completed, operations were then transferred from Cargo Lion to its new subsidiary for licensing reasons, while a second DC-8 was taken on strength. After delivery of the aircraft, which was equipped with Stage III-compliant hushkits, a Luxembourg identity was allocated before it entered service on long-term contracts for Lufthansa and British Airways.

Throughout this period the administration requirements had steadily grown in accommodation at Ostend that had not expanded in sympathy. It was therefore a convenient point to move the overflowing corporate offices to Luxembourg to meet the requirements of the country's Civil Aviation Authority. A suitable building at Findel Airport was identified for development, but delays meant that the airline had to maintain two operating bases until the building work was completed in 1997. A third DC-8-62 entered service in mid-1998, mainly flying ad hoc charters until its reliability had been proved. In the same year Cargo Lion was also contracted to fly passenger charters for the first time using an Airbus A310 on behalf of Air France's subsidiary Air Charter. This operation also led to a similar four-month contract from Transavia in the 1998 summer season.

In early 1999 one DC-8 was flying for DHL, one employed on Air Afrique's link between West Africa and central Europe, while L'Aéropostale employed the third for its night mail flights around France, a short-term contract that was expected to be extended. In April the company signed a Letter of Intent to acquire two DC-10-30Fs to further increase its available capacity. Both are former British Airways machines which will be converted by Aeronavali in Italy before delivery in November 1999 and July 2000.

Fleet (Cargo):

Regn	*Srs*	*C/n*	*Regn*	*Srs*	*C/n*
Airbus A310			LX-TLC	62F	45920
LX-TXA	324	594	**Douglas DC-10**		
Douglas DC-8			LX-	30F	-
LX-TLA	62F	45960	LX-	30F	-
LX-TLB	62F	45925			

Cargolux (CV/CLX)

Head Office: Findel Airport, L-2990 Luxembourg, Luxembourg
Tel: (352) 4211 3366 Fax: (352) 4211 3411

Cargolux was formed in March 1970 with the assistance of Loftleidir Icelandic, Luxair, the Salen Shipping Co of Sweden and a group of private investors. Operations began in September with a trip to Hong Kong using a single 24-ton-capacity Canadair CL-44 (TF-LLJ) acquired from Loftleidir. A second example (TF-LLG) from the same source joined the fleet in August 1970, but its career was short-lived as it crashed in Bangladesh in December. Two more examples of the type were introduced into the fleet in 1972 as Cargolux continued to develop the cargo market from its Luxembourg base. Although it was 1978 before the last of the turboprop type had been phased out, towards the end of 1973 the first DC-8 was leased which marked the start of a new era for the company. Such was the volume of traffic through Findel, that a new cargo terminal was completed in 1976, by which time Cargolux was operating three DC-8s.

Following the delivery of its first Boeing 747, Cargolux began regular transatlantic cargo services to the US eastern seaboard in January 1979, in so doing becoming the first European airline to operate the dedicated freighter variant. By the mid-1980s the Luxembourg carrier had six Boeing 747s on strength, having phased out the DC-8 equipment in 1984. By this time the company had become one of the top 15 cargo airlines in the world, a position that was to further improve in the next few years. Cargolux became the first company to introduce the freighter version of the 747-400 towards the end of 1993, with nine more specimens due to follow at regular intervals. It is now Europe's largest scheduled all-freight airline, regularly serving a large number of destinations around the world.

To maintain this level of business it was necessary to have an equally efficient support facility, so in 1996 a new cargo centre was inaugurated in Luxembourg. The 500,000 tons-capacity unit is now one of Europe's most modern cargo facilities. Early in 1999 Cargolux announced its plans to float the company on the Stock Exchange later in the year, with the aim of raising up to $150 million to fund further expansion of the Boeing 747 fleet. Both Luxair and Swissair have about a 30% shareholding in the airline, but this will be diluted to some 25% by the flotation. Nevertheless, the freight carrier achieved good results in 1998 with a net profit of $92 million on revenues of $578 million. Utilisation of the 747s is amongst the highest in the industry, the aircraft averaging nearly 16 hours per day in the air. Further evidence of its success will become apparent later in 1999 when Cargolux expects to take delivery of the world's first 747-400F simulator.

Below: Although Cargolux still operates the Boeing 747 LX-DCV it has been reregistered N809MC with Atlas Air and leased back. *AJW*

Fleet (Cargo):

Regn	Srs	C/n
Boeing 747		
LX-FCV	4R7F (SCD)	25866
LX-GCV	4R7F (SCD)	25867
LX-ICV	428F (SCD)	25632
LX-KCV	4R7F (SCD)	25868
LX-LCV	4R7F (SCD)	29053
LX-MCV	4R7F (SCD)	29729
LX-NCV	4R7F (SCD)	29730
LX-OCV	4R7F (SCD)	29731
LX-PCV	4R7F (SCD)	29732
LX-RCV	4R7F (SCD)	29733

Note: Somewhat confusingly Cargolux tends to reuse registrations to retain the CV content of the identity.

Cathay Pacific Cargo (CX/CPA)

Head office: Swire House, 9 Connaught Road, Central, Hong Kong
Tel: (852) 27 47 50 00 Fax: (852) 28 10 65 63

Cathay was created in 1946 equipped with one DC-3, gradually growing throughout the next three decades until in July 1979 the company introduced its first Boeing 747. Although a passenger-carrying variant, it provided considerable capacity in the underfloor holds for additional cargo. Later Cathay acquired its first dedicated 747 freighter which had served with British Airways until 1982. Its introduction greatly increased the airline's cargo carrying capability, which was further improved by the arrival of a 747-400 freighter in 1994. The Hong Kong-based carrier was the first Asian operator to employ the variant which can lift a payload of 122 tons. The cargo fleet is kept busy with regular flights to London and Frankfurt, while North America and Australia are also frequently visited. In terms of cargo tonnage handled Cathay features amongst the world's top 10.

Fleet (Cargo):

Regn	*Srs*	*C/n*
Boeing 747		
B-HIH	267F (SCD)	23120
B-HVX	267F (SCD)	24568
B-HVY	236F (SCD)	22306
B-HVZ	267F (SCD)	23864
B-HUH	467F (SCD)	27175
B-HUK	467F (SCD)	27503

Challenge Air Cargo (WE/CWC)

Head Office: PO Box 523979, Miami, Florida 33122, USA
Tel: (305) 869 83 33 Fax: (305) 869 82 99

In the mid-1980s there was a distinct reduction in the number of airlines that were offering dedicated freight services between the US and Latin America despite the expansion of the latter's flower industry. This encouraged the creation of several new carriers, with Miami a popular choice as the US gateway. One such airline was Challenge Air Cargo which was founded in 1985 as a subsidiary of Challenge Air Transport, although this association ended after one year.

Initially freight charters were operated between Miami, Central and South America and the Caribbean using piston-engined DC-6s and former military C-46 Commandos. It did not take long for the business to flourish, which enabled the airline to replace the elderly equipment with the necessary larger and more modern types such as the DC-8 and Boeing 707. Towards the end of the decade Challenge had become one of the leading cargo airlines, carrying an annual volume of goods valued in excess of $100 million. The growth continued into the 1990s, by which time the carrier had developed its activities to such an extent that it was one of the leading scheduled all-cargo operators. New Boeing 757-200Fs had been acquired, each offering 15 pallet positions within a capacious interior. Nowadays Challenge moves a wide range of cargo from Latin America, but specialises in transporting seafood, vegetables, flowers and horses. It added its first wide-bodied equipment during 1998 following the delivery of two ex-Japan Airlines DC-10s after their conversion into freighters. By the spring of 1999 the three 10-year-old 757s were becoming too small for the company's expanding market presence, so the decision was taken to replace them with a similar number of DC-10-40s for delivery in July 1999, November 1999 and February 2000. All are former Japan Airlines machines and will be converted to freighters before joining the US company. However, before these events took place, in June 1999 it was announced that UPS had acquired the operational assets of Challenge including the carrier's significant Latin America traffic rights. These included 13 destinations, plus 17 in North America, but the transaction did not involve the Challenge fleet. In fact, it was expected that the DC-10s and Boeing 757s would be operated on a wet-lease basis for UPS in the immediate future. However, in the longer term there is every possibility that the airline will continue to operate independently, although the loss of the lucrative scheduled routes could present difficulties.

Above: Boeing 757-23APF N573CA is operated by Challenge Air Cargo and was the one-time G-OBOZ with Anglo Airlines. *K. Buchanan via G. Pennick*

Fleet (Cargo):

Regn	*Srs*	*C/n*	*Regn*	*Srs*	*C/n*
Boeing 757			**Douglas DC-10**		
(To be withdrawn by February 2000)			N140WE	40F	46920
N571CA	23APF	24456	N141WE	40F	46661
N572CA	23APF	24868	N142WE	40F	46966
N573CA	24APF	24971	N606GC	30F	47929
			N	40F	-

Channel Express (LS/EXS)

Head Office: Building 470, Bournemouth International Airport, Christchurch, Dorset BH23 6SE
Tel: (01202) 59 33 44 Fax: (01202) 57 35 12

When this company began operations in 1978 it was known as Express Air Services with its equipment comprising a small fleet of Handley Page Heralds. These were used for frequent freight flights to the Channel Islands, with freshly-cut flowers making up the loads for the return journeys. At the start of the carrier's career the aircraft were used for weekend passenger charters over the same routes, but this activity was soon discontinued.

In 1983 the Channel Express identity was adopted and having acquired some Post Office mail contracts, the number of Heralds operated for this work and ad hoc charters steadily increased. In the early 1990s a modernisation programme was instigated to upgrade and refurbish most of the fleet to so-called Super Herald standard, an undertaking that produced a considerable improvement in performance by the aircraft. Although the type continued to serve the airline faithfully, eventually it was necessary to consider a replacement. As a result, from the mid-1990s there was a gradual phasing-out of the Heralds in favour of the Fokker F-27 Friendship 500/600 until G-BEYF became the final example of the veteran to be retired in the spring of 1999. Although the Dutch-built machine originated in the same era, it is faster, quieter and offers a greater range with an increased payload.

A need for more capacity over longer sectors was responsible for Channel Express evaluating a number of larger types in the late 1980s. This led to the introduction of several Lockheed Electras that had already been converted for freight duties in the US. The modifications included the installation of a forward cargo door 11ft 3in x 6ft 11in (343cm x 211cm) giving the type compatibility with the wide-bodied equipment. Channel uses the Electras for both domestic and international services, the containerised loads allowing much faster turn-rounds, an all-important feature of night mail and parcel operations.

During 1997 the airline took delivery of its first Airbus A300B4 after its conversion to a freighter by BAe Aviation Services at Bristol/Filton. It subsequently began regular flights between Tel Aviv and Stansted on behalf of British Airways in addition to charter work for a number of companies. It was soon confirmed that the A300 was an ideal choice for a medium-sized freighter and by mid-1998 Channel had three examples in its fleet.

Meanwhile the visits to the Channel Islands continue although flowers are no longer carried by the aircraft. Instead they are transported in the company's climate-controlled lorries operated by the haulage division.

Above: Arrival at Stansted for the A300 G-CEXC after another cargo sortie. *AJW*

Below: Now that the Heralds have been retired, the short-range freight work is handled by seven F-27s. *A. S. Wright*

Below: Loading the Electra G-OFRT through its rear cargo door. *Channel Express*

Left: Cargo of assorted shapes and sizes being loaded into the Channel Express A300 G-CEXC. *Channel Express*

Left: The A300-103F can carry a maximum payload of 99,200lb (45,000kg) in its vast maindeck which accommodates various configurations of pallets and containers. *Channel Express*

Fleet:

Regn	*Srs*	*C/n*
Airbus A300B4		
G-CEXC	103F	124
G-CEXH	203F	117
G-CEXI	203F	121
(operates for TNT)		
Fokker F-27 Friendship		
G-BNIZ	600	10405
G-CEXA	500	10503
G-CEXB	500	10550
G-CEXD	600	10351
G-CEXE	500	10654
G-CEXF	500	10660
G-JEAP	500	10459
Lockheed Electra		
G-BYEF	L188CF	2006
G-CEXS	L188CF	1091
G-CHNX	L188AF	1068
G-OFRT	L188CF	1075
N285F	L188AF	1107
N360Q	L188CF	1112

(G-JEAP leased from JEA, Electras N341HA and N343HA also leased when required)

China Airlines (CI/CAL)

Head Office: 131 Nanking East Road, Section 3, 104 Taipei, Taiwan
Tel: (2) 27 15 22 33 Fax: (2) 27 17 51 20

China Airlines was formed in 1958 as a domestic carrier with two aircraft leased from the military. An international route to Saigon was opened in the 1960s, while the company became the official flag carrier for Taiwan in 1965. The China Aviation Development Foundation took the airline public in 1993 when it was listed on the Taiwan Stock Exchange.

Some years earlier in 1982 China Airlines began serving Luxembourg in partnership with the airport's resident airline Cargolux. The destination became the only European gateway for the Far East carrier's weekly dedicated Boeing 747 cargo services which were doubled in frequency in 1989. The demand continued to grow in the next decade which necessitated further adjustments to the operation in 1995. European destinations now include Amsterdam and Frankfurt in addition to Luxembourg.

The Taiwan carrier is now preparing for the anticipated growth in the freight industry by planning to order 13 Boeing 747-400 freighters. Subject to the receipt of approval from the country's Ministry of Transportation and Communications, CAL will place the order with Boeing with deliveries starting in 2000. The carrier will then begin to retire its existing fleet of ageing Series 200s.

Fleet:

Regn	*Srs*	*C/n*
Boeing 747		
B-160	209F (SCD)	24308
B-18751	209B (SCD)	21454
B-18752	209F (SCD)	22299
B-18755	209B (SCD)	22447
N518MC	243B (SCD)	23476
N528MC	2D7B (SCD)	22472

City Bird (H2/CTB)

Head Office: Building 117D, Melsbroek Airport, B-1820 Melsbroek, Belgium
Tel: (2) 752 52 11 Fax: (2) 752 52 10

Since operations began in March 1997, City Bird has specialised in low-cost, long-haul, scheduled passenger services from Brussels to various transatlantic destinations.

However, on 26 November 1998 it was announced that the company had ordered two Airbus A300-600s for delivery in June and July 1999, to become the first dedicated freight aircraft to be operated by the carrier. The pair were originally built for Kuwait Airways, but the order was subsequently not taken up, hence the early delivery slot available for the Belgian airline.

City Bird hopes to gain some of the freight traffic that at present is being taken by road to other airports such as Amsterdam, Frankfurt, Luxembourg, Paris and Milan for onward travel to distant destinations. Initially the airline planned to employ the A300s mainly on intra-European flights, but it is also intended to develop routes to the Far East, South America and South Africa.

An agreement has been reached with Lignes Aériennes Congolaises (LAC) which

Fleet:

Regn	*Srs*	*C/n*
Airbus A300-600		
OO-CTT	C4-605R	755
OO-CTU	C4-605R	758
Boeing 747		
OO-	400F	-
OO-	400F	-

City Bird also operates three MD-11s and two Boeing 767-300ERs for passenger services.

will result in the Belgian carrier introducing a dedicated cargo service between Brussels and Kinshasa. The long-haul services will be flown by two Boeing 747-400F freighters ordered from Boeing and due for delivery in mid-2000. In the meantime City Bird is considering the possible lease of two 747-200Fs pending the arrival of its own aircraft.

CLA Air Transport (C9/CXX)

Head Office: PO Box 7419, Domestic Airport Post Office, Manila 1301, Philippines
Tel: (2) 551 71 92 Fax: (2) 552 74 21

This new cargo carrier that was formed in March 1997 originally aimed to launch its dedicated freight scheduled services by the end of January 1999, but operations had to be postponed due to the difficulty in gaining slots at Tokyo (Narita). The Philippine Aerospace Development Co has a 51% shareholding in the company, with the remaining 49% held by the Japanese ground handler IASS. A single DC-8 leased from Arrow Air was intended to be used by the carrier for flights linking Manila and Cebu with Tokyo and Osaka Kansai.

Fleet:

Regn	*Srs*	*C/n*
Douglas DC-8		
N345JW	63AF	46042

Continental Cargo Airlines (CCL)

Head Office: 364-366 Kensington High Street, London W14 8NS
Tel: (171) 602 7055 Fax: (171) 603 5533

Continental operates services on behalf of GM Airlines, itself a subsidiary of General Mediterranean Holding. The flights are carried out within Africa and to various European destinations.

Fleet:

Regn	*Srs*	*C/n*	*Regn*	*Srs*	*C/n*
Boeing 707			9G-ADS	323C	19587
9G-ADM	321C	19369			

Coyne Airways (7C/COY)

Head Office: Rofel House, Colet Gardens, Hammersmith, London W14 9DH
Tel: (0181) 563 8811 Fax: (0181) 563 8822

Founded in 1990, the company specialises in air cargo shipments to the CIS, Central Asia and the Middle East. The equipment employed mainly comprises eastern European-built types such as the Antonov An-124, An-12 and Ilyushin Il-76 freighters that are leased and chartered as required. These aircraft are ideal for bulk cargoes since they are usually equipped with an onboard crane, which facilitates operations into airports possessing little or no handling equipment on site. Western-built aircraft are largely excluded from these CIS sorties for this reason.

Coyne has exclusive agreements with a number of airlines in the CIS which helps when traffic rights are needed to any part of the continent. In recent times the company has been able to offer a service for part loads and general cargo to a number of destinations around the Caspian Sea. A hub has been created in Baku which is served by scheduled and chartered Il-76s every week. Onward transportation by air is available to Aktau, Atyrau, Ashkhabad and Tbilisi if required.

DAS Dairo Air Services (SE/DSR)

Head Office: 30 Jinja Road, Kampala, Uganda. European Office: ANA House, Aviation Court, Gatwick Road, Crawley, West Sussex RH10 2RJ
Tel: (01293) 54 03 03 Fax: (01293) 55 15 45

Formed in 1983 as Uganda's all-cargo airline, the company uses the name DAS Air Cargo for operational purposes. Flights began in 1984 by employing a Boeing 707 for freight charters that linked Africa with Europe. When more examples of the type were acquired in 1993 the company was able to offer worldwide charters with its fleet of hush-kitted machines. Each aircraft can carry 13 pallets of main deck cargo in addition to the underfloor holds which are useful for fresh vegetables, fruit and flowers. These originate from a wide variety of African locations with Gatwick and Amsterdam frequently the destination. Considerably more capacity became available in 1995 when DAS introduced the first of two Douglas DC-10-30s. This had served for many years with Sabena as OO-SLA with several short spells on lease to other carriers. Reregistered 5X-JOE with its latest owner, the trijet was joined by N400JR in November 1997 after its conversion into a dedicated freighter.

Fleet:

Regn	*Srs*	*C/n*	*Regn*	*Srs*	*C/n*
Boeing 707			**McD Douglas DC-10**		
5N-ARQ	338C	18809	5X-JOE	30F	47906
5X-JEF	379C	19821	N400JR	30F	46976
5X-JET	351C	19411	N800WR	30F	46955

DHL Worldwide Express (ER/DHL)

Head Office: PO Box 75122, Cincinnati, OH 45275, USA
Tel: (606) 283 22 32 Fax: (606) 525 19 98

The identity of the company is derived from the initials of the three founders: Dalsey, Hillbloom and Lind. It was created in 1969 as a courier service, ferrying shipping papers to the Middle and Far East and throughout the Pacific region to Hawaii. Comprising Hong Kong-based DHL International and San Francisco-based DHL-US, the company soon became the leading worldwide small package carrier. At first the consignments were flown on scheduled services, but as expansion continued apace in the 1970s, DHL began to charter its own dedicated small freighters.

Domestic services began in 1981 with the nightly shipments sorted at the company's main hubs in Cincinnati and Salt Lake City, although it was not long before 12 such centres were in use. However, unlike competitors such as FedEx and UPS, DHL does not specifically target the US market where the business handled represents only 25% of the total revenue.

DHL Airways was established as the operating arm of DHL Worldwide Express

Above: A number of carriers are contracted to DHL for feeder services, the Spanish company Swiftair being the operator of this SA226AT Merlin registered EC-GBI which is leased from European Air Transport but flown in DHL colours. *AJW*

Above: European Air Transport operates a large fleet of Boeing 727s for DHL work, this example being OO-DHX. *AJW*

Below: DHL operates DC-8s for its trunk routes, the Series 73AF N805DH at one time being Air Canada's C-FTIS. *AJW*

and now has access to a large fleet of aircraft spread around the world. Many of these are chartered small freighters which help to move over 150,000 shipments through the main US hub each night. There are also daily links with the Brussels hub run by the DHL company European Air Transport. This airline wet-leases its equipment which comprises a mix of Boeing 727s and Convair 580s, all being flown in the US company's livery. The growing need for larger capacity machines has resulted in EAT and DHL placing orders for a number of Airbus A300 freighters for both the European network and the US domestic system. These will replace the DC-8s in the latter case, but the type will still continue with the regular transatlantic sorties in the short term. However, there is a limit to its ability to cope with the loads, especially since the company transports over 130,000kg across the Atlantic every night. It appears likely that DHL will need to acquire a small fleet of Boeing 747 freighters to provide more capacity in the not too distant future.

Fleet:

Regn	*Srs*	*C/n*
Airbus A300B4		
N361DH	103F	071
N	103F	084
N	103F	085
N	203F	141
N	203F	149
N366DH	203F	249
N367DH	203F	265
Boeing 727		
N622DH	264F	20896
N623DH	264F	20895
N624DH	264F	20709
N625DH	264F	20780

Regn	Srs	C/n	Regn	Srs	C/n
N626DH	277F	22644	N724DH	228F	19862
N627DH	277F	22641	N726DH	228F	20409
N701DH	30C	19011	N727DH	228F	20204
N702DH	30C	19793	N740DH	2Q9F	21930
N703DH	30C	19010	N741DH	2Q9F	21931
N705DH	22C	19191	N742DH	225F	21290
N706DH	22C	19192	**Douglas DC-8**		
N707DH	22F	18321	N801DH	73F	46033
N708DH	25F	18275	N802DH	73F	46076
N709DH	82C	19968	N803DH	73F	46123
N712DH	29F	19401	N804DH	73F	46124
N715DH	155C	19618	N805DH	73F	46125
N717DH	23F	19389	N806DH	73CF	46002
N720DH	228F	19544	N807DH	73CF	45990
N721DH	228F	19545	N873SJ	73CF	46091
N722DH	228F	19861			

EgyptAir (MS/MSR)

Head Office: Cairo International Airport, Cairo, Heliopolis, Egypt
Tel: (2) 245 4400 Fax: (2) 390 1557

Founded as Misr Airwork in June 1932, the Egyptian airline started operations one year later. In 1949 the carrier became Egyptian-owned and adopted the title Misair for a time, but after an agreement had been reached between Syria and Egypt in 1958, United Arab Airlines (UAA) was created. This arrangement only lasted until

Above: EgyptAir has two A300s configured for cargo work, one being SU-BDG. *A. S. Wright*

Fleet (Cargo):

Regn	Srs	C/n	Regn	Srs	C/n
Airbus A300			**Boeing 747**		
SU-BDG	B4-203F	200	SU-GAL	366 (SCD)	24161
SU-GAC	B4-203F	255	SU-GAM	366 (SCD)	24162

1961 when Syria ended its participation, leaving its partner to continue as UAA. However, three years later in 1964, Misr was revived although only for domestic operations. Finally the two airlines were combined in October 1971 under the title of EgyptAir.

A varied collection of types have subsequently been operated by the airline with cargo handled by Boeing 707s, 747-300 combis and two Airbus A300s configured as dedicated freighters.

El Al Cargo (LY/ELY)

Head Office: PO Box 41, Ben-Gurion International Airport, 32 Ben Yehuda Street, Tel Aviv
Tel: (3) 971 61 11 Fax: (3) 972 14 42

Since its creation in 1948 El Al has grown into a major carrier using modern equipment for its passenger and freight services. The latter commenced in 1975 with a convertible version of the Boeing 747 which was soon joined by a second example. Later in the decade a third aircraft was acquired by the cargo division, this time a former Continental machine which had been converted for freight work. Finally a dedicated freighter entered service with El Al in 1979 to join the remainder of the fleet on the busy European and transatlantic flights. This machine (4X-AXG) was lost in 1992 when the aircraft crashed into a block of flats during its departure from Amsterdam. For many years the Israeli Government was the majority shareholder of the airline, but in 1996 it was privatised. Strangely, El Al still suffers from a rule that prevents operations on the Jewish Sabbath which is of course to the advantage of competitors. This also applies to El Al Cargo which wet-leases a Boeing 747 to rival CAL Cargo Airlines when required.

Above: El Al has several Boeing 747s for freight carrying, 4X-AXD being a combi version. *AJW*

Fleet:

Regn	*Srs*	*C/n*	*Regn*	*Srs*	*C/n*
Boeing 747			4X-AXK	257F (SCD)	22151
4X-AXD	258C	21190	4X-AXL	257F (SCD)	22150
4X-AXF	258C	21594	4X-AXZ	124F (SCD)	19735
4X-AXH	258B (SCD)	22254			

Emerald Airways (G3/JEM)

Head Office: South Terminal, Speke Hall Avenue, Liverpool Airport, Merseyside L24 1YW
Tel: (0151) 448 08 44   Fax: (0151) 448 05 49

When established at Southend in December 1987 the company was known as Janes Aviation after its founder. Operations began in the following summer using a single Britten-Norman Islander for regular flights between Blackpool and Belfast City under contract to Lynx Express. The volume of work quickly brought the need for larger equipment, resulting in a Trislander and several DC-3s joining the fleet, although the latter were replaced by a Short SD3-30 after a brief time. This proved to be a more efficient machine for the duties that involved regular sorties across the Irish Sea to the Isle of Man, Eire and Belfast. For a period in the early 1990s a pair of Handley Page Heralds were also leased, but towards the end of 1991 the airline began its association with the HS748.

The first specimen to arrive was G-BPDA which had served in a passenger role with the short-lived Chieftain Airways and Scottish European. The type quickly proved ideally suited to the cargo work envisaged, so Janes began to collect more from various sources around the world, including six from the former Dan-Air fleet. It was not long before the airline possessed the largest fleet of HS748s in Europe, consequently enabling the company to secure more valuable contracts. These included the nightly movement of mail and parcels for the Post Office, newspaper flights and express courier services.
By this time all of these operations were flown from Liverpool, since in June 1993 the airline decided to move its headquarters from Blackpool to the Merseyside airport. The relocation also provided the opportunity to change the airline's name to Emerald Airways, an identity chosen to reflect the amount of business carried out across the Irish Sea. Although essentially a cargo carrier, in September 1994 the company decided to

Fleet:

Regn	*Srs*	*C/n*	*Regn*	*Srs*	*C/n*
HS748			G-BGMO	2A	1767
G-ATMI	2A	1592	G-BIUV	2A (SCD)	1701
G-ATMJ	2A	1593	G-BPDA	2A	1756
G-AVXI	2A	1623	G-BVOU	2A	[illegible]
G-AVXJ	2A	1624	G-BVOV	2A	1777
G-AYIM	2A	1687	G-OPFW	2A	1714
G-BEJD	1	1543	G-OSOE	2A	1697
G-BGMN	2A	1766	G-SOEI	2A	1689

Below: Although essentially a dedicated cargo airline, Emerald had a short spell with limited passenger services in 1998; HS748 G-EMRD was one of two aircraft employed for such work before being transferred to South Africa in mid-1999. *AJW*

diversify into the passenger market with scheduled services between Liverpool and the Isle of Man commencing in April 1996. These were maintained by a pair of 748s configured with 48 seats, with another two aircraft available for rapid conversion if required. However, in early 1999 Emerald announced that it was ending its involvement with scheduled passenger flights in view of disappointing traffic figures. Undoubtedly the presence of Manx on the route provided strong competition that was difficult to counter.

Emery Worldwide Airlines

(EB/EWW)

Head Office: 1 Lagoon Drive, Redwood City, California 94065, USA
Tel: (415) 596 96 00 Fax: (415) 596 96 11

Although formed in 1946, the company operated as the Emery Air Freight division of the world's largest freight forwarding organisation until late 1981. Airline operations had begun a year earlier by Emery Air Freight, following years of service using aircraft chartered from other carriers. The original operating hub was at Smyna, Tennessee, but this was moved to a new $50 million centre at Dayton, Ohio in 1981.

Consolidated Freightways was merged with Emery in 1989 which attracted a vast number of customers and a contract from

Fleet:

Regn	*Srs*	*C/n*
Boeing 727		
N7635U	222F	19908
N7638U	222F	19911
N7639U	222F	19912
N7640U	222F	19913
N7642U	222F	19915
N7643U	222F	20037
N7644U	222F	20038
N7645U	222F	20039
Boeing 747		
N	-	-
N	-	-
Douglas DC-8		
N105WP	73F	46095
N500MH	71F	45812
N602AL	73F	45991
N603AL	73F	46003
N604AL	73F	46047
N605AL	73F	46106
N606AL	73F	46044
N791FT	73CF	46045
N792FT	73CF	46046
N795FT	73CF	46103
N796FT	73CF	46104
N796AL	63F	46054
N797AL	63CF	46163
N801GP	71F	46039
N811AL	71F	46099
Regn	*Srs*	*C/n*
N831AL	73F	46149
N832AL	73F	46063
N865F	63CF	46088
N870TV	73CF	46086
N921R	63CF	46145
N950R	63CF	45903
N951R	63AF	46092
N957R	63CF	46137
N959R	63CF	46143
N961R	73F	46133
N964R	63F	46000
N990CF	62F	46068
N991CF	54F	45801
N992CF	54F	45884
N993CF	62F	46028
N994CF	62F	45956
N995CF	62F	46024
N996CF	62F	46162
N997CF	62F	46154
Regn	*Srs*	*C/n*
N998CF	62F	46139
N2674U	73F	46062
N8076U	71F	45941
N8079U	71F	45947
N8084U	71F	45974
N8085U	71F	45975
N8087U	71F	45977
N8091U	71F	45995

Regn	Srs	C/n	Regn	Srs	C/n
N8177U	71F	45983	N68043	10F	46902
Douglas DC-10			N68044	10F	46903
N68041	10F	46900	N68046	10F	47800
N78042	10F	46901	N68047	10F	47801

Below: Emery Worldwide employs a large fleet of assorted DC-8s. *A. S. Wright*

the US Postal Service to carry mail and parcels over a number of routes radiating from the hub at Indianapolis. In addition to its mail work, Emery Worldwide also operates international express charters and now serves more than 95 countries worldwide. In 1999 the company acquired two Boeing 747s for its guaranteed delivery service which was launched in January 1999. It was planned for one of the aircraft to operate from Los Angeles for the benefit of Californian clients, while its partner was allocated to the southeast USA and Puerto Rico using Raleigh NC as its base. Emery was also due to receive the first of six DC-10-10s in April 1999 with deliveries of the remainder spread over the next two years or so.

Ethiopian Airlines (ET/ETH)

Head Office: PO Box 1755, Addis Ababa, Ethiopia
Tel: (1) 61 22 22 Fax: (1) 61 14 74

Although formed as the national state-owned carrier in 1946, it was 1958 before the airline began regular cargo flights with three DC-6s. These were used to develop a number of routes in Africa, particularly to the Sudan, Nigeria, Liberia and Ghana. During the company's early years it received much assistance from TWA, the US carrier continuing this support to the 1970s. It enabled Ethiopian to expand its freight involvement, especially from 1968 when a pair of convertible Boeing 707s were taken on strength to replace the DC-6s on the cargo services.

The arrival of the jets made some significant expansion possible, with the type's longer range enabling sorties to be operated to London and China. Short-range trips later became the responsibility of a pair of DHC-5 Buffalos, while the two Boeing 767-200s that were added to the fleet in the mid-1980s each provided 12 tons of underfloor cargo capacity. Later, the introduction of two Lockheed Hercules in 1988 gave the airline the ability to operate to the more remote and short landing strips even with a load of 23 tons. It also became the first African carrier to acquire a Boeing 757 freighter which was delivered in 1990.

Fleet:

Regn	Srs	C/n
Boeing 757		
ET-AJS	260PF	24845
Boeing 767		
ET-AIE	260ER	23106
ET-AIF	260ER	23107
ET-AKW	33AER	25346
ET-ALC	33AER	28043

Regn	Srs	C/n
DHC-5D Buffalo		
ET-AHJ	-	102
Lockheed L-100 Hercules		
ET-AJK	30	5022
ET-AKG	30	5306

European Air Transport (QY/BCS)

Head Office: Building 4-5, Brussels International Airport, B-1930, Zaventem, Belgium
Tel: (2) 718 14 14 Fax: (2) 718 15 55

The company was founded in December 1971 as a flying training school employing seven instructors. During the next few years over 800 pilots were trained, but in the mid-1970s this activity ended with the company's decision to operate commercial passenger services. The first contract it secured was with Sabena in 1976 and involved the provision of flights to Cologne, Dusseldorf, Eindhoven and Luxembourg from the Belgian capital. Before a start could be made it was necessary to acquire a suitable machine for the task, which resulted in three Swearingen Metros joining the company. With the trio carrying the flag carrier's livery, EAT became the first charter company in Europe to operate the type. The airline gained an enviable reputation for time-keeping during this period which probably did not go unnoticed by DHL when developing its European operation because EAT became a subsidiary of the US small package carrier in 1986. Gradually a fleet of Convair 580s were delivered to Brussels, all being repainted in DHL livery before entering service. Subsequently converted Boeing 727s were introduced and more recently the first of the ordered Airbus A300s has entered service. Under DHL ownership EAT has played a major part in its parent's European operations.

Fleet:

Regn	Srs	C/n
Airbus A300B4		
OO-DLC	203F	152
OO-DLD	203F	259
OO-DLE	203F	238
OO-DLF	203F	208
Boeing 727		
OO-DHK	277F	22643
OO-DHM	31C	20114
OO-DHN	31C	20113
OO-DHO	31C	20112
OO-DHR	35F	19834
OO-DHS	223F	20189
OO-DHT	223F	19489

Regn	Srs	C/n
OO-DHU	223F	20992
OO-DHV	223F	21084
OO-DHW	223F	20993
OO-DHX	223F	20994
OO-DHY	223F	20905
OO-DHZ	2Q4F	22424
OO-DLB	277F	22642
Convair 580		
OO-DHC	-	68
OO-DHE	-	52
OO-DHF	-	147
OO-DHL	-	459

All in DHL colours

EVA Air (BR/EVA)

Head Office: EVA Building, 376 Hsinan Road, Sec 1, Luchu, Taoyuan Hsien, 338, Taiwan
Tel: (3) 351 5151 Fax: (3) 351 0005

Although established in March 1989 by the Evergreen shipping line, another two years passed before operations began on 1 July 1991. The delay was caused by a variety of reasons, one being the similarity of the name with other companies. The airline also had to wait for its aircraft to be delivered, the first being a pair of Boeing 767-300ERs intended for passenger services around the Far East. The network at the time of the launch included links from Taipei to Bangkok, Jakarta, Kuala Lumpur, Seoul and Singapore.

The fleet received a pair of Boeing 747s in November 1992, an event that allowed the introduction of the first European service to Vienna, later extended to Heathrow in the following April. With the arrival of more 747s, the airline was able to operate them in a combined freight/passenger configuration, attracting much traffic destined for the European markets. With the success of the cargo division, EVA decided to convert its order for six passenger MD-11s so that half of them were delivered as dedicated freighters. The first sortie by one of the latter was operated between Taiwan and Amsterdam in October 1995, with other routes soon added. The type has since proved very reliable and by the end of 1999 the airline planned to have nine examples of the variant on strength with another three for dedicated passenger work.

Fleet:

Regn	*Srs*	*C/n*
Boeing 747 (passenger)		
B-16401	45E	27062
B-16402	45E	27063
B-16410	45E	29061
B-16411	45E	29111
B-16412	45E	29112
Boeing 747 (SCD combi)		
B-16461	45E	27154
B-16462	45E	27173
B-16463	45E	27174
B-16465	45E	26062
N403EV	45E	27141
N405EV	45E	27142
N406EV	45E	27898
N407EV	45E	27899
N408EV	45E	28092
N409EV	45E	28093
McD Douglas MD-11F (freight)		
B-16106	AF	48545
B-16107	AF	48546
B-16108	AF	48778
B-16109	AF	48779
B-16110	AF	48786
B-16111	AF	48787
B-16112	AF	-
B-16113	AF	-
N105EV	AF	48544

Four Boeing 767-200s and four 767-300ERs are operated in passenger configuration.

Evergreen International Airlines (EZ/EIA)

Head Office: 3850 Three Mile Lane, McMinnville, Oregon 97128-9496, USA
Tel: (503) 472 00 11 Fax: (503) 434 42 10

Although Evergreen can trace its history back to Johnson Flying Service of 1924, it was only in 1975 that it emerged in its present form as a division of Evergreen Aviation. The latter also owns Evergreen Helicopters, one of the largest of its kind in the US. Towards the end of 1975 the airline opened an office in Washington DC to liaise with US government agencies for additional operating authority. As a result a contract was acquired to fly services for the USAF using three convertible DC-9-32Fs for the purpose. Evergreen also purchased three DC-8-52s formerly with Air New Zealand for international charter work which included the 1977 programme of pilgrim flights between Nigeria and Mecca.

Above: Evergreen has reduced its Boeing 727 fleet although N731EV is still on strength. *A. S. Wright*

During 1978 the airline was successful in its bid to obtain a contract from the US Military Airlift Command which necessitated the addition of a DC-8-61F to the fleet. Meanwhile the company also provided a scheduled cargo service linking Seattle with Oakland and Los Angeles using Electras for this operation. There was some significant expansion in the early 1980s when Evergreen introduced the first of a large fleet of Boeing 727 freighters dedicated to a UPS contract relating to the overnight movement of parcels. A number of DC-8-73s were also flown for the same customer, supplementing a growing collection of secondhand Boeing 747s which were employed for long-haul charters or wet- leasing to other carriers around the world. In the mid-1990s the fleet was reduced in size and variety leaving DC-9s and Boeing 747s to handle all operations.

Fleet:

Regn	*Srs*	*C/n*	*Regn*	*Srs*	*C/n*
Boeing 747			**Douglas DC-9**		
N470EV	273C	20653	N915F	15F	47061
N471EV	273C	20651	N916F	15F	47044
N472EV	131 (SCD)	20320	*Regn*	*Srs*	*C/n*
N474EV	121 (SCD)	19637	N932F	32F	47355
N477EV	SR-46 (SCD)	20784	N933F	33F	47191
N478EV	SR-46 (SCD)	21033	N935F	32F	47220
N479EV	132 (SCD)	19898	N940EV	33F	47414
N480EV	121 (SCD)	20348	N944F	33F	47194
N481EV	132 (SCD)	19896	N945F	33F	47279
N482EV	212B (SCD)	20713			
N485EV	212B (SCD)	20712			

Express Airways (EPA)

Head Office: Flughaven Hahn, Geb 417, D-55483 Lautzenhausen, Germany
Tel: (6543) 98 73 00 Fax: (6543) 987 30 33

A member of the Farnair Europe Group, Express Airways was formed in 1998 to provide freight services in Europe. In 1999 it received the first of eight Short SD3-60s which the company is to operate under contract to FedEx for the latter's European network. A further four examples of the type were due to be allocated to the Hahn-based carrier later in the year.

Fleet (Cargo):

Regn	*Srs*	*C/n*	*Regn*	*Srs*	*C/n*
Fokker F27			**Short SD3-60**		
D-AAAC	500	10448	See under Farnair Europe		

Express One International

(EO/LHN)

Head Office: 3890 West Northwest Highway,
Suite 70C Dallas, Texas 75220, USA
Tel: (972) 902 2501 Fax: (972) 350 1399

When formed in 1975 the airline was known as Jet East International, adopting the present name in 1989. Its early career was spent as an air taxi operator from Dallas Love Field using a mix of Beech King Airs and Learjets. By 1980 the company had decided to enter the airline business, securing a number of Boeing 727s after obtaining a contract from United Parcel Service, followed later by similar employment on behalf of DHL and Emery. The regular work for the courier companies kept Express One busy, but nevertheless the airline began to diversify into passenger charter operations. By this time DC-9s had joined the fleet in 1991, while two years later the first transatlantic charter was operated using one of two leased DC-10-30s for a sortie to Frankfurt.

Express One suffered a setback in June 1995 when a routine inspection by the FAA generated some concerns about safety

Fleet:

Regn	*Srs*	*C/n*
Boeing 727		
N15DF	264F	20710
N230NE	31F	18907
N240NE	31F	18906
N275WC	277F	20549
N290NE	25F	18972
N300NE	25F	18974
N352PA	225F	20616
N357NE	82F	19405
N368PA	221F	22540
N721RW	2M7	21200
N742RW	2M7	21952
N6813	223F	19488
N6815	223F	19490
N6819	223F	19494
N6826	223F	19704
N6839	223F	20192
N12305	231F	19562
N68782	232F	20637
N74318	231F	20051
Douglas DC-9		
N934VJ	31	48114
N943VJ	31	47058
N945VJ	31	47066
N950VJ	31	47564
N959VJ	31	47352
N969VJ	31	47421

Above: The Express One Boeing 727 N6815 is one of several leased to Brussels-based European Air Transport for its express parcels business. *AJW*

checks. The airline promptly grounded its fleet voluntarily and at the same time sought the US Chapter 11 protection from creditors while some reorganisation of the airline's affairs was undertaken. Once this was completed Express One resumed operations with a smaller fleet, using it to fulfil contracts from the US Postal Service that involved night operations at Indianapolis. Other ad hoc domestic charters were also flown, while international successes included the award of a contract from DHL to link its Brussels hub with various European destinations including the UK.

Farnair Europe (FRN)

Head Office: PO Box 12059, NL-3004 GB Rotterdam, Netherlands
Tel: (10) 437 81 00 Fax: (10) 437 21 64

Formed in 1997, the company is an alliance between Tulip Air of the Netherlands, Farner Air Transport Switzerland, Express Airways from Germany, MiniLiner Italy and Farner Air Transport Hungary. Scheduled express cargo sorties and ad hoc charters are operated and feeder services to the mainline carriers are also contracted. A fleet of former US-registered Short SD3-60s was acquired in early 1999 for use on the FedEx local services in Europe.

Fleet:

Regn	*Srs*	*C/n*
Airbus A300		
PH-CLA	B4-103F	044
PH-EAN	B4-103F	041
PH-GIR	B4-103F	042
Fokker F-27		
D-AAAC	500	10448
HB-ILQ	500	10389
HB-ISQ	500	10447
HB-ISY	500	10370
PH-FNV	500	10397
PH-FNW	500	10398
PH-FOZ	500	10425
PH-JLN	500	10449
Short SD3-60		
D-CFAO	300	SH3734
D-CFDX	300	SH3725
D-CFXA	300	SH3754
D-CFXB	300	SH3756
D-CFXC	300	SH3744
D-CFXD	300	SH3749
D-CFXE	300	SH3733
D-CFXF	300	SH3740

Above: The A300 PH-EAN is operated by the Farnair Europe Group in DHL's full livery. *A. S. Wright*

Fast Air Carrier (UD/FST)

Head Office: Cargo Terminal, Arturo M. Benitez Airport, Santiago, Chile
Tel: (2) 601 94 30 Fax: (2) 601 97 01

Founded in January 1978, Fast Air specialises in the domestic and international air freight business. Owned by the Cueto family and Boris Hirmas, the airline is a part of the same group as LAN Chile. As a result the latter's cargo contracts are handled by its subsidiary when necessary, with most of the work involving visits to American destinations in the North and South. European services are operated to Frankfurt normally, although in the past two years a short season of flights in the run-up to Christmas has seen Fast Air carrying cargoes of grapes into Stansted. Even the current uprisings in Chile failed to affect the arrival of the fruit for the 1998 festive season. The airline acquired a minority interest in the Miami-based freight carrier Florida West during 1995, the company having a similar network of routes to that of Fast Air.

Fleet:

Regn	*Srs*	*C/n*
Boeing 747		
N293AE	2B4B (SCD)	21098
N617FF	121 (SCD)	19650
Douglas DC-8		
CC-CAR	71F	45976

Federal Express (FedEx) (FX/FDX)

Head Office: PO Box 727, Memphis, TN 38194-2424, USA
Tel: (901) 369 3600 Fax: (901) 332 3772

Federal Express began its successful career in June 1971, although it was April 1973 before the first flight was operated by one of the company's large fleet of Dassault Falcon 20s. Initially the aircraft used bases at Burbank, Los Angeles and San Diego

Above: After Federal Express was established in the US, the company turned its attention to Europe in 1985, using three modified Boeing 727s for the nightly service linking Memphis with Brussels and Stansted. One of the aircraft was N219FE, a machine that is still in service but no longer required to make the long crossing. *AJW*

with which a wide selection of US cities were linked. The machines were modified for the duties by installing a large cargo door for easy handling of the small packages, but by the early 1980s the rapid growth of the industry meant that the Falcons were too small for the loads. Deregulation of the US cargo operations was largely responsible, with the result that in 1978 FedEx began collecting former passenger-carrying Boeing 727s for conversion into dedicated freighters.

The company decided to set up a central hub at Memphis, Tennessee, where the consignments were sorted for onward distribution. Expansion continued unabated with an international network joining the original domestic operations. European flights were introduced which for a time used specially modified Boeing 727s for the transatlantic runs, but the type was soon replaced by DC-10s and later MD-11s. By taking over Flying Tigers in 1989, the company acquired South American and transpacific access in addition to a number of Boeing 747s and DC-8s. In the mid-1990s FedEx received the first of a batch of 30 Airbus A300-600s which were also joined by 39 A310s purchased from carriers including Lufthansa, KLM and Swissair specifically for freighter conversion.

A similar programme was conceived to update the carrier's vast DC-10 fleet, which not only involves the passenger to freight modification, but also includes the installation of the advanced MD-11 flightdeck for two crew members rather than the DC-10's normal complement of three. Such is the degree of change that the aircraft will become known as MD-10s under an amended type certificate and include former Srs 10s and Srs 30s retired by such as United and American Airlines. Yet despite the overall size of the fleet, a significant number of small airlines are contracted to fly services into the hubs, between them using mainly some 260 Cessna Caravans and 32 Fokker Friendships. Up to 12 Short SD3-60s were expected to be introduced into the European network during 1999 and operated by Express Airways of the Farnair Europe Group on behalf of FedEx.

FedEx has also played a large part in the specification of the new Ayres LM200

Above: FedEx still has a number of Boeing 727s based in Europe to handle feeder traffic, the Series 21C N144FE on this occasion operating from Basle. *AJW*

Loadmaster, becoming a launch customer with an initial order for 50 aircraft. Designed for single pilot operation, it will carry four LD3 cargo containers and be employed by FedEx for feeder traffic. Ayres aimed to fly the prototype towards the end of 1999, a year or so later than originally planned. Hopefully certification of this specialist type will be achieved by the end of 2000.

The popularity of the Boeing 727 as a freighter has not waned through the years, but the forthcoming Stage 3 noise regulations has meant that in order for the machines to continue flying profitably into the next century, some upgrading work has had to be implemented. FedEx therefore devised a Stage 3 Kit to meet the noise standards demanded at a fraction of the cost of re-engining or new replacement aircraft. Unlike some other systems, there is no degraded take-off thrust, reduced field performance, changes in operating procedures or the manufacturer's wing design. The company has since received over 700 orders from more than 60 owners and operators worldwide for the kit which is fully certified for all 727 variants. It was also developed with the full collaboration of Pratt & Whitney and technical support from Boeing.

Since FedEx began operations there have been many imitators but the carrier has remained in its position as the world's largest transportation company. With over 625 aircraft and 42,500 road vehicles in use worldwide the situation is extremely unlikely to change.

Fleet:

Regn	*Srs*	*C/n*	*Regn*	*Srs*	*C/n*
Airbus A300			N658FE	605F	752
N650FE	605F	726	N659FE	605F	757
N651FE	605F	728	N660FE	605F	759
N652FE	605F	735	N661FE	605F	760
N653FE	605F	736	N662FE	605F	761
N654FE	605F	738	N663FE	605F	766
N655FE	605F	742	N664FE	605F	768
N656FE	605F	745	N665FE	605F	769
N657FE	605F	748	N667FE	605	771

Above: Nowadays FedEx employs its MD-11s for the regular missions to Europe, one of which has just been completed by N607FE. *AJW*

Regn	*Srs*	*C/n*	*Regn*	*Srs*	*C/n*
N668FE	605	772	N408FE	203F	257
N669FE	605	774	N409FE	203F	273
N670FE	605	777	N410FE	203F	356
N671FE	605	778	N411FE	203F	359
N672FE	605	779	N412FE	203F	360
N673FE	605	780	N413FE	203F	397
N674FE	605	781	N414FE	203F	400
N675FE	605	789	N415FE	203C	349
N676FE	605	790	N416FE	222F	288
N677FE	605	791	N417FE	222F	333
N678FE	605	792	N418FE	222F	343
N679FE	605	793	N419FE	222F	345
N680FE	605	794	N420FE	222F	339
N681FE	605	799	N421FE	222F	342
N682FE	605	800	N422FE	222F	346
N683FE	605	801	N423FE	203F	281
N684FE	605	802	N424FE	203F	241
N685FE	605	803	N425FE	203F	264
N686FE	605	804	N426FE	203F	245
Airbus A310			N427FE	203F	362
N401FE	203F	191	N428FE	203F	248
N402FE	203F	201	N429FE	203F	364
N403FE	203F	230	N430FE	203F	394
N404FE	203F	233	N442FE	203F	353
N405FE	203F	237	N443FE	203F	283
N407FE	203F	254	N445FE	203F	297

Above: Turn-rounds of the MD-11s are quickly completed. *A. S. Wright*

Regn	Srs	C/n
N446FE	222F	224
N447FE	221F	251
N448FE	221F	260
N449FE	221F	217
N450FE	221F	162
N451FE	221F	303
N452FE	221F	313

Boeing 727

Regn	Srs	C/n
N101FE	22C	19197
N102FE	22C	19193
N103FE	22C	19199
N104FE	22C	19198
N105FE	22C	19194
N106FE	22C	19201
N107FE	22C	19202
N112FE	22C	19890
N113FE	22C	19894
N114FE	24C	19527
N116FE	25C	19298
N117FE	25C	19299
N118FE	25C	19300
N119FE	25C	19301
N120FE	25C	19356
N124FE	25C	19360
N127FE	25C	19719
N128FE	25C	19720
N133FE	25C	19851
N134FE	25C	19852
N135FE	25C	19853
N136FE	25C	19855
N143FE	21C	19136
N144FE	21C	19137
N145FE	27C	19109
N146FE	27C	19110
N147FE	22F	19080
N148FE	22F	19086
N149FE	225	19087
N150FE	22F	19141
N151FE	22F	19147
N152FE	25F	18285
N154FE	25F	18287
N155FE	25F	18288
N156FE	25F	18289
N166FE	22F	18863
N167FE	22F	18864
N168FE	22F	18865
N169FE	22F	18866
N181FE	22F	18868
N184FE	22F	18870
N185FE	22F	18871
N186FE	22F	18872
N187FE	22F	19079
N188FE	22F	19081
N189FE	22F	19082
N190FE	22F	19083
N191FE	22F	19084
N193FE	22F	19142
N194FE	22F	19143
N195FE	22F	19144
N196FE	22F	19145
N198FE	22F	19154
N199FE	173C	19509
N201FE	2S2F	22924
N203FE	2S2F	22925
N204FE	2S2F	22926
N205FE	2S2F	22927
N206FE	2S2F	22928
N207FE	2S2F	22929
N208FE	2S2F	22930
N209FE	2S2F	22931
N210FE	2S2F	22932
N211FE	2S2F	22933
N212FE	2S2F	22934
N213FE	2S2F	22935
N215FE	2S2F	22936
N216FE	2S2F	22937
N217FE	2S2F	22938
N218FE	233F	21101
N219FE	233F	21102
N220FE	233F	20934
N221FE	233F	20932
N222FE	233F	20933
N223FE	233F	20935
N233FE	247F	21327
N234FE	247F	21328
N235FE	247F	21329
N236FE	247F	21330
N237FE	247F	21331
N240FE	277F	20978
N241FE	277F	20979
N242FE	277F	21178
N243FE	277F	21480
N244FE	277F	21647
N245FE	277F	22016
N246FE	277F	22068
N254FR	233F	20936
N257FE	233F	20939
N258FE	233F	20940
N262FE	233F	21624
N263FE	233F	21625
N264FE	233F	21626
N265FE	233F	21671
N266FE	233F	21672

Regn	Srs	C/n	Regn	Srs	C/n
N267FE	233F	21673	N469FE	225F	21581
N268FE	233F	21674	N477FE	227F	21394
N269FE	233F	21675	N478FE	227F	21395
N270FE	233F	22035	N479FE	227F	21461
N271FE	233F	22036	N480FE	227F	21462
N272FE	233F	22037	N481FE	227F	21463
N273FE	233F	22038	N482FE	227F	21464
N274FE	233F	22039	N483FE	227F	21465
N275FE	233F	22040	N484FE	227F	21466
N276FE	233F	22041	N485FE	227F	21488
N277FE	233F	22042	N486FE	227F	21489
N278FE	233F	22345	N487FE	227F	21490
N279FE	233F	22346	N488FE	227F	21491
N280FE	233F	22347	N489FE	227F	21492
N281FE	233F	22348	N490FE	227F	21493
N282FE	233F	22349	N491FE	227F	21529
N283FE	233F	22350	N492FE	227F	21530
N284FE	233F	22621	N493FE	227F	21531
N285FE	233F	22622	N494FE	227F	21532
N286FE	233F	22623	N495FE	227F	21669
N287FE	2D4F	21849	N496FE	227F	21670
N288FE	2D4F	21850	N497FE	232F	20866
N461FE	225F	22548	N498FE	232F	20867
N462FE	225F	22550	N499FE	232F	21018
N463FE	225F	22551	N502FE	25F	18271
N464FE	225F	21288	N503FE	25F	18273
N465FE	225F	21289	N504FE	25F	18274
N466FE	225F	21292	N505FE	25F	18276
N467FE	225F	21449	N506FE	25F	18277
N468FE	225F	21452	N507FE	25F	18278

Above: Seen in the company's 1980s/1990s scheme, FedEx DC-10-30 N303FE arrives at Stansted at the end of a daily transatlantic crossing. *AJW*

Regn	Srs	C/n
N508FE	25F	18279
N509FE	25F	18280
N510FE	25F	18282
N511FE	25F	18283

Boeing 747

Regn	Srs	C/n
N636FE	245F (SCD)	21764
N638FE	245F (SCD)	21841
N639FE	2R7F (SCD)	21650
N640FE	245F (SCD)	20826

Douglas DC-10/MD-10

Regn	Srs	C/n
N301FE	30F	46800
N302FE	30F	46801
N303FE	30F	46802
N304FE	30F	46992
N305FE	30F	47870
N306FE	30F	48287
N307FE	30F	48291
N308FE	30F	48297
N309FE	30F	48298
N310FE	30F	48299
N311FE	39F	46871
N312FE	30F	48300
N313FE	30F	48311
N314FE	30F	48312
N315FE	30F	48313
N316FE	30F	48314
N317FE	30F	46835
N318FE	30F	46837
N319FE	30F	47820
N320FE	30F	47835
N321FE	30F	47836
N322FE	30F	47908
N364FE	10F	46600
N365FE	10F	46601
N366FE	10F	46602
N367FE	10F	46605
N368FE	10F	46606
N369FE	10F	46607
N370FE	10F	46608
N371FE	10F	46609
N372FE	10F	46610
N373FE	10F	46611
N374FE	10F	46612
N375FE	10F	46613
N377FE	10F	47965
N384FE	10F	46617
N385FE	10F	46619
N386FE	10F	46620
N387FE	10F	46621
N388FE	10F	46622
N390FE	10F	46624
N391FE	10F	46625
N392FE	10F	46626
N395FE	10F	46629
N397FE	10F	46631
N10060	10F	46970
N40061	10F	46973

Above: When converted to a freighter such as N480FE, the Boeing 727 has a large loading door to assist speedy turn-rounds. *A. S. Wright*

Regn	Srs	C/n
N68048	10F	47802
N68049	10F	47803
N68050	10F	47804
N68051	10F	47805
N68052	10F	47806
N68053	10F	47807
N68054	10F	47808
N68056	10F	47810
N68057	10F	48264
N68058	10F	46705
N68059	10F	46907

McD Douglas MD-11

Regn	Srs	C/n
N581FE	AF	48419
N582FE	AF	48420
N583FE	AF	48421
N584FE	AF	48436
N585FE	AF	48481
N586FE	AF	48487
N587FE	AF	48489
N590FE	AF	48505
N601FE	AF	48401
N602FE	AF	48402
N603FE	AF	48459
N604FE	AF	48460
N605FE	AF	48514
N606FE	AF	48602
N607FE	AF	48547
N608FE	AF	48548
N609FE	AF	48549
N610FE	AF	48603
N611FE	AF	48604
N612FE	AF	48605
N613FE	AF	48749
N614FE	AF	48528
N615FE	AF	48767
N616FE	AF	48747
N617FE	AF	48748
N618FE	AF	48754
N619FE	AF	48770
N620FE	AF	48792
N621FE	AF	48792
N623FE	AF	48794

Short SD3-60

See under Farnair Europe

Fine Air (FB/FBF)

Head Office: 1649 NW 62 Avenue, PO Box 523726, Miami, Florida 33152, USA
Tel: (305) 871 55 55 Fax: (305) 871 4232

Miami-based Fine Air received its operating certificate in 1992 enabling operations to begin on 10 November. As a scheduled cargo carrier, the airline concentrated its attention on South and Central America plus the Caribbean area and now has links with over 23 cities on a regular basis. As in the case of a number of similar carriers in the region, Fine Air leases equipment to other companies from time to time.

The airline suffered a setback on 7 August 1997 when it lost DC-8-61F N27UA during a take-off crash at Miami International. As a result Fine Air voluntarily suspended operations during some intensive checks by the FAA investigation team, but the carrier was hopeful of a restart within 30 days. In the event authorisation to recommence flying came on 28 October, by which time the company had implemented the newest and safest cargo loading procedures in the country. It was expected that other freight airlines in the US would follow the lead by also introducing the system.

Despite its relatively short career, Fine Air now has more than 1,200 customers worldwide, a figure certain to increase following intensive marketing. The company is already one of the leading international air cargo carriers in South Florida with the most scheduled flights, the greatest frequencies and the largest number of destinations. Plans are in hand to meet the demand by increasing the number of markets served, while the fleet will be expanded with wide-bodied types. The longer range and increased capacity will allow the airline to serve more distant countries in South America and ultimately transatlantic cities.

In fact, Fine Air introduced its first wide-bodied freighter into commercial service early in 1999. The converted ex-LTU TriStar 200 will be used to serve various South American destinations from the carrier's hub at Miami. It was also announced that the company had taken over Arrow Air and its operations although it is expected that the aircraft will continue to carry the latter's titles initially.

Fleet:

Regn	Srs	C/n	Regn	Srs	C/n
Douglas DC-8			N427FB	54F	45684
N29UA	61F	46159	N505FB	51F	45410
N30UA	61F	45888	N508DC	51F	45935
N44UA	54F	45800	N7046H	54F	46011
N54FA	54F	45637	N8008D	51F	45252
N55FB	55F	45678			
N56FA	54F	45663	**Lockheed L-1011 TriStar**		
N57FB	54F	45669	N260FA	200F	1158
N426FB	54F	45667			

First Air (7F/FAB)

Head Office: 3257 Carp Road, Carp, Ontario KOA 1LO, Canada
Tel: (613) 839 3340 Fax: (613) 839 5690

The company has a long history dating back to its launch in 1946 as Bradley Air Services. A varied collection of aircraft are employed, the airline division operating under the name of First Air. Freight services are flown to the regions in the north of Canada and also to Greenland. In fact it is not unknown for a First Air Boeing 727 to cross the Atlantic, but these are usually passenger charters. In order to accommodate such business the aircraft are operated as combis with seating arranged as required.

Fleet:

Regn	Srs	C/n	Regn	Srs	C/n
Boeing 727			C-GXFA	233C	20938
C-FIFA	225F	20381			
C-FRST	90C	19169	**Boeing 737**		
C-FUFA	233F	20941	C-FNVT	248C	21011
C-GFRB	27C	19120			
C-GOFA	35C	18815			
C-GVFA	44C	20475			

A number of Twin Otters and HS748s are also operated.

First International Airways

Head Office: Ostend Airport, B-8400 Ostend, Belgium
Tel: Not available Fax: Not available

A new cargo carrier set up in 1998 for the purpose of operating between Ghana and its European base at Ostend. As is the usually the custom with African companies, it is equipped with some elderly Boeing 707s, but in addition has the much travelled CL-44-0 Conroy Guppy on strength after its spell with AZAL Avia Cargo of Azerbaijan. Upon its return it was resident at Southend for maintenance for some time, but eventually crossed the Channel in May 1999.

Fleet:

Regn	Srs	C/n	Regn	Srs	C/n
Boeing 707			9G-OOD	399C	19415
9G-FIA	331C	20069			
9G-OLD	324C	19350	**Conroy CL-44**		
			9G-LCA	0	16

Florida West International Airways (RF/FWL)

Head Office: PO Box 026752, Miami, Florida 33102-5752, USA
Tel: (305) 871 77 80 Fax: (305) 871 77 81

The airline can trace its history back to 1981 when Pan Aero International began cargo services based at Miami. The name Florida West Airlines was adopted in 1984 at a time when the carrier was flying both domestic and international freight charters using a large fleet of Boeing 707s. Despite holding some valuable contracts to operate charters for the US Military Airlift Command, the company was forced into bankruptcy in 1992 which brought an end to all operations. The aircraft were repossessed or sold, but eventually a new owner was found for the airline which then became known as Florida West International Airways. All of the assets and the subsidiary companies of the earlier organisation were included in the $3.5 million sale, which marked the restart of operations in March 1996.

Fleet:

Regn	*Srs*	*C/n*
Douglas DC-8		
N161DB	61F	45980

Gemini Air Cargo (GR/GCO)

Head Office: 12020 Sunrise Valley Drive, Reston 20191-3429, Virginia, USA
Tel: (703) 391 01 00 Fax: (703) 391 09 85

The airline was developed from Potomac Capital which was a small leasing company in the US. In this capacity the company endeavoured to find a home for six former Lufthansa DC-10s that were in the process of conversion to pure freighters in 1994. Unfortunately no potential customers could be found for the machines which were nevertheless in excellent condition after their passenger careers with the German flag carrier. There was little alternative for Potomac than to form its own airline with the equipment already available. Gemini was therefore launched in 1995 with the first flight taking place in December. The

Above: Gemini Air Cargo has been building up a fleet of DC-10-30s that are suitable for freighter conversion. Lufthansa has been the source for most of the additions with N600GC previously registered D-ADMO with the German carrier. *A. S. Wright*

airline began to offer wet-lease charters with some success and soon had two aircraft dedicated to Swissair's requirements. Other satisfied clients have included Alitalia, British Airways, Fast Air, Finnair and KLM, with the arrangements varying from part-time wet-leases to longer duration contract charters. Obviously when the major carriers are in need of capacity or a back-up aircraft they expect reliability and dependability from the provider, otherwise failure soon looms.

During 1997 Gemini began a six-times-weekly scheduled service from Seoul to New York JFK and was subsequently able to sell space on a regular basis to several Far East customers. For the future the carrier hopes to expand its fleet of DC-10s up to 20 aircraft spread over the next three years or so. This growth has been made possible by the major US investor, The Carlyle Group, taking a majority stake in the carrier in mid-1999. Gemini has already successfully acquired three more examples of the trijet that were recently retired by British Airways, with the freighter conversion entrusted to the Italian company Aeronavali for completion during the first three months of 2000.

In addition to this development, the airline is expected to announce that it intends to introduce the MD-11F, the extra capacity to be offered to both new and existing customers. In the meantime Gemini has been awarded a long-term contract by China Eastern for a DC-10.

Above: As the DC-10 has been retired by passenger carriers, so the type has become increasingly popular as a freighter, with several contractors specialising in the conversion programme.
A. S. Wright

Fleet:

Regn	*Srs*	*C/n*	*Regn*	*Srs*	*C/n*
McD Douglas DC-10			N605GC	30F	47925
N600GC	30F	46965	N606GC	30F	47929
N601GC	30F	47921	N607GC	30F	46978
N602GC	30F	47923	N	30F	46921
N603GC	30F	47922	N	30F	46932
N604GC	30F	47924	N	30F	47840

HeavyLift Cargo Airlines

(NP/HLA)

Head Office: Stansted Airport, Stansted, Essex CM24 1QW
Tel: (01279) 68 06 11 Fax: (01279) 68 16 63

When TAC HeavyLift was launched in 1980 freight airlines were experiencing the effects of the current world recession. A number had already ceased trading, including Trans Meridian Air Cargo with which the newcomer had lingering ties. The company's choice of the Short Belfast was unusual since the well proven CL-44 and Hercules were readily available, but the former RAF transport was considered to be superior for the type of work envisaged. This proved to be the case, although not before much time and money had been spent on the modifications called for by the CAA.

Once the certificate had been issued in March 1982, customers were found for the Belfasts, many from within the air transport industry. In fact the movement of helicopters and large airliner sections became a frequent undertaking for the Stansted-based carrier, which also operated the one-off Conroy CL-44-0, another type capable of handling unusual cargo. During the first half of the 1990s the fleet included a Boeing 707 for general freight work, but eventually this was sold.

In September 1988 HeavyLift became a wholly-owned subsidiary of Trafalgar House, the UK-based international group engaged in commercial and residential property, construction and engineering, passenger and cargo shipping together with hotels. Eight years later in 1996, Trafalgar House was itself taken over by Kvaerner PLC, the Norwegian group with similar interests.

In the meantime there had been a major development with the setting up of a joint venture with the Ukrainian company Volga Dnepr. As a result of this co-operation, six (later increased to seven) examples of the enormous Antonov An-124 freighters became available for worldwide operations, two normally being based at Stansted. With a payload of 120 tonnes, the aircraft are in constant use although their weight and size can cause parking problems. HeavyLift also has access to a pair of Ilyushin Il-76s, another useful large-capacity type.

During 1997 the company became a launch customer for the Airbus A300B4

Above: HeavyLift still finds plenty of employment for its two Belfasts of which G-BEPS is one example. *AJW*

freighter conversion, three examples of which were in service by the end of 1998. The former passenger airliner rapidly proved to be an ideal aircraft for regional routes in Europe, the eastern Mediterranean and North Africa. Its ability to carry full-size maindeck pallets and a payload of 45 tonnes also makes it a good feeder type for the long-haul scheduled operators. HeavyLift's first customer was

Above: The Antonov An-124 can cope with enormous loads and seven of the type are operated by Volga-Dnepr in association with HeavyLift. *HeavyLift*

Above: Containers that are more at home on lorries or ships create no problems for loading into the An-124's spacious hold, since the aircraft has its own on-board crane. *AJW*

Fleet:

Regn	Srs	C/n
Airbus A300B4		
G-HLAA	203F	047
G-HLAB	203F	045
G-HLAC	203F	074
G-HLAD	203F	154
Antonov An-12B		
RA-12995	-	00347402
Antonov An-124		
RA-82042	100	9773054055093
RA-82043	100	9773054155101
RA-82044	100	9773054155109
RA-82045	100	9773052255113
RA-82046	100	9773052255117
RA-82047	100	9773053259121
RA-82078	100	9773054559153
Ilyushin IL-76		
RA-76369	TD	1033414480
RA-76842	TD	1033418616
Short SC5 Belfast		
G-BEPS	-	SH1822
G-HLFT	-	SH1819

KLM Cargo, the latter extending its existing five-year agreement. After delivery in October 1997, the A300 took over the Dutch company's five-nights-per-week Amsterdam-Stockholm service plus an additional daytime run on Sundays. It also undertakes weekly flights for KLM to link Amsterdam with Bologna, Italy and Zaragoza in Spain, although some of this work was transferred to Schreiner Airways in 1999.

Above left: Because of its size parking the An-124 can produce a few problems. *AJW*

Below left: Several Hercules were leased by HeavyLift for special contracts in the early 1990s. *HeavyLift*

Hunting Cargo Airlines

(AG/ABR)

See Air Contractors (Ireland)

Iberia Cargo (IB/IBE)

Head Office: 130 Calle Velazquez, E-28006 Madrid, Spain
Tel: (1) 587 87 87 Fax: (1) 587 58 84

Iberia formed a cargo subsidiary in 1988 under the name of Cargosur which thereafter operated the flag carrier's medium/long-range freight flights on a wet-lease basis. This continued until 1995 when the airline was integrated into the parent company and the aircraft were repainted in the latter's livery.

Fleet:

Regn	*Srs*	*C/n*	*Regn*	*Srs*	*C/n*
Boeing 747			**Douglas DC-8**		
EC-DLC	256B (SCD)	22454	EC-EMD	62F	46023
EC-DLD	256B (SCD)	22455	EC-EMX	62F	45921
EC-EEK	256B (SCD)	24071	EC-FVA	71F	45945

ICC Air Cargo Canada (CIC)

Head Office: 780 Magenta Boulevard, Farnham, Quebec J2N 1B8, Canada
Tel: (450) 293 3656 Fax: (450) 293 5169

Formed in 1986, the Canadian company Air Charter Systems (ACS) assembled a fleet of three Douglas DC-8s with which to commence its proposed worldwide freight services. These duly began, continuing for six years or so before the company sold the elderly trio, but although this left the airline without equipment, it continued in business by leasing DC-8s whenever needed. Interestingly, one of the carrier's original machines (C-FIWW) was acquired by MK Airlines, which provides a daily African link with the UK.

In 1997 preparations were made for the arrival of an Airbus A300 freighter after it had been converted at Bristol/Filton. It was in fact the third airframe to receive the treatment and was rolled out on 9 November. After making its maiden flight in ACS's full livery on 26 November, it was stored pending delivery across the Atlantic. This did not take place for some time, but eventually the aircraft was ferried from Bristol to Toronto on 16 October 1998, still carrying ACS titles. These were subsequently removed following a change of name by the company which is now operating as ICC Air Cargo Canada with a fleet of two A300s with two more examples of the type on order. One of the fleet operates under contract to Emery Worldwide but remains Canada-based to operate services between its home country and the US carrier's hub at Dayton, Ohio.

Fleet:

Regn	*Srs*	*C/n*	*Regn*	*Srs*	*C/n*
Airbus A300			C-	B4-203F	101
C-FICA	B4-203F	023	C-FICI	B4-203F	173
C-FICB	B4-203F	078			

JAL Cargo (JL/JAL)

Head Office: 2-4-11Higashi-Shinagawa, Shinagawa-ku, Tokyo 140, Japan
Tel: (3) 54 60 31 91 Fax: (3) 54 60 59 29

Japan Airlines (JAL) was formed in August 1951 as a private company, with operations starting a few months later with a flight from Tokyo to Osaka in October. At first the activities were confined to domestic services using equipment and staff leased from Northwest Airlines, a US carrier already prominent in the Far East. At this time JAL was not allowed to employ Japanese nationals as aircrew under the terms of the Allied Peace Treaty, but during this period the company was able to plan its future policy. Some reorganisation in 1953 found the airline 50%-owned by the Government, leaving the remainder with private sources. It also marked the start of international operations once again, with traffic rights granted between Tokyo and the USA.

Cargo services were launched in 1959 using a new Douglas DC-7 freighter to link Tokyo with San Francisco on a weekly basis. During the 1960s this type was withdrawn and replaced by a pair of DC-8-55s, one configured for mixed passenger and freight working. JAL was in the forefront of operators from the beginning of the wide-body era and by the early 1980s had 40 Boeing 747s on strength, four of which were freighters. At this point JAL Cargo was already the leading international freight carrier in terms of revenue per kilometres flown, a success assisted by the pioneering use of Russian air space for the European services. From November 1987 the Japanese flag carrier became a private company once again following the sale of the Government's remaining shareholding.

Fleet:

Regn	*Srs*	*C/n*	*Regn*	*Srs*	*C/n*
Boeing 747			JA8165	221F (SCD)	21743
JA811J	246F (SCD)	22989	JA8171	246F (SCD)	23391
JA8123	246F (SCD)	21034	JA8180	246F (SCD)	23641
JA8132	246F (SCD)	21681	JA8193	212B (SCD)	21940
JA8160	221F (SCD)	21744	JA8937	246F	22477

JHM Cargo Express (JHM)

Head Office: 1 Santa Maria Airport, 2nd Piso, San Jose, Costa Rica
Tel: (305) 871 2355 Fax: (305) 871 6016

JHM is a relatively new airline which was formed in 1997 with the intention of operating cargo flights to the Americas and the Caribbean area. Approval was sought and received from the Costa Rican authorities and it was hoped to start up as soon as similar permission was given by the US. The company had noted a shortage of reliable scheduled services for exporters from the territory, so after careful evaluation of the prospects, seven former Alitalia Airbus A300s were acquired on lease from C-S Aviation Services. These were due to join the company at regular intervals after conversion to freight configuration by British Aerospace at Bristol/Filton.

Fleet:

Regn	Srs	C/n	Regn	Srs	C/n
Airbus A300			N68142	B4-203F	142
N59106	B4-203F	106	N	B4-203F	101
N59107	B4-203F	107	N	B4-203F	139
N59140	B4-203F	140	N	B4-203F	173

Kalitta American International Airways (CB/CKS)

See Kitty Hawk International

Kitty Hawk Air Cargo (KR/KHA)

Head Office: PO Box 612787, Dallas Fort Worth International Airport, Texas 75261, USA
Tel: (972) 456 6000 Fax: (972) 456 2277

The airline was founded as Kitty Hawk Airways in 1976 to operate both passenger and cargo flights. Subsequently freight has become the main occupation of the company, one of the few with scheduled services dedicated solely to air freight forwarders both domestic and international. Kitty Hawk can handle all types of loads using either container, pallet or bulk shipping to accommodate all shapes and sizes. The airline operates a route network embracing 28 major US cities through its hub at Terre Haute, Indiana, with over 24 other cities served by a road feeder service. In 1985 the airline merged with the companies of Christopher Charters whereby the Kitty Hawk Group was created. Twelve years later the latter merged with the Kalitta companies in 1997 but retained its identity.

Fleet:

Regn	Srs	C/n	Regn	Srs	C/n
Boeing 727			N6809	223F	19484
N587CA	-	463	N6810	223F	19485
N90AX	222F	20040	N6811	223F	19486
N180AX	222F	20041	N6812	223F	19487
N252US	251F	19971	N6816	223F	19491
N255US	251F	19974	N6821	223F	19496
N264US	251F	19983	N6827	223F	20180
N270AX	90C	19170	N6831	223F	20184
N278US	251F	21157	N6833	223F	20186
N279US	251F	21158	N6834	223F	20187
N281KH	2J0F	21105	N6838	223F	20191
N284KH	2J0	21108	N69739	224F	20667
N727CK	22C	19195	N69740	224F	20668
N750US	214F	21512	N79746	224F	22449
N751US	214F	21513			
N854AA	223F	20995	**Convair 600**		
N855AA	223F	20996	N94205	-	10
N856AA	223F	20997	N94226	-	48
N858AA	223F	21085	N94246	-	102
N6806	223F	19481	N94258	-	119
N6807	223F	19482	N94279	-	101
N6808	223F	19483			

Regn	Srs	C/n	Regn	Srs	C/n
Convair 640			**Douglas DC-9**		
N860FW	-	10	N112PS	15F	47013
N866TA	-	283	N561PC	15F	47014
N3412	-	32	N562PC	15F	47012
			N563PC	15F	47055
			N564PC	15F	47062

Kitty Hawk International
(CB/AIT)

Head Office: 842 Willow Run Airport,
Ypsilanti, Michigan 48198, USA
Tel: (734) 484 0088 Fax: (734) 484 3630

In March 1999 it was announced that Pacific Aviation Logistics had agreed to sell its 40% interest in Kalitta American International Cargo (AIC) to Kitty Hawk, already the holder of a 60% stake in the company. Now a wholly owned subsidiary, AIC will continue its successful scheduled service linking Los Angeles with Honolulu which is believed to fly more than 45% of the total freight carried between the two cities. A weekly trip by AIC around the Pacific Rim has also continued to produce steady volumes throughout the downturn in Asian economics, the destinations

Fleet:

Regn	Srs	C/n	Regn	Srs	C/n
Boeing 727			N708CK	269B (SCD)	21543
N4735	235F	19455	N709CK	132 (SCD)	20247
Boeing 747			N710CK	2B4F (SCD)	21097
N701CK	146 (SCD)	19725	N712CK	2B4F (SCD)	21098
N702CK	146 (SCD)	20332	N713CK	2B4F (SCD)	21099
N703CK	146 (SCD)	19727	**Douglas DC-8**		
N704CK	146 (SCD)	20528	N24UA	61C	45963
N706CK	238B (SCD)	20010	N801CK	55F	45816
N707CK	269B (SCD)	21541			

Below: Freighters are often seen in an all-white colour scheme as is the case of the Kitty Hawk International Boeing 747 N713CK. *AJW*

Regn	*Srs*	*C/n*
N801MG	62F	45986
N802CK	54F	45679
N801MG	62F	46098
N803CK	62F	46085
N804CK	51F	45689
N805CK	51F	45649
N806CK	54F	45932
N807CK	55F	45767
N808CK	55F	45817
N809CK	55F	45803
N810CK	52F	45814
N811CK	63CF	46147
N812CK	61F	45890
N813CK	61F	45893
N814CK	62F	45986
N815CK	63F	46151
N816CK	61F	45892
N817CK	61F	45887
N818CK	62CF	45961
N819CK	62F	46098
N6161C	55F	45856
N6161M	55F	45762
N8052U	54F	46009
Lockheed L-1011 TriStar		
N102CK	200F	1198
N103CK	200F	1212
N104CK	200F	1193
N105CK	200F	1178
N106CK	200F	1211
N107CK	200F	1182
N108CK	200F	1204
N109CK	200F	1205
N110CK	50F	1132
N112CK	50F	1146

including Hong Kong, Melbourne and the Hawaiian Islands.
The airline was originally formed in 1965 as Connie Kalitta Services based at Willow Run from where charter services were flown for the local motor industry. The carrier progressed to DC-8s in the mid-1980s, steadily expanding both fleet and route network in this period, at the same time gaining official approval to operate internationally. In the early 1990s the American International Airways title was adopted, the company subsequently ordering an initial five TriStar 200s for freighter conversion by Marshall Aerospace at Cambridge UK.

KLM Cargo (KL/KLM)

Head Office: PO Box 7700, 1117 ZL Schiphol Airport-Oost, Netherlands
Tel: (20) 649 91 23 Fax: (20) 41 28 72

Formed in October 1919, the Dutch national carrier can truly claim to be the oldest airline in the world that has retained the same name throughout its existence. From the outset the company showed an interest in air freighting, however modest the loads. Only a small proportion of KLM's revenue was earned by cargo traffic, yet the company continued to be optimistic for the future prospects. By 1960 the airline was amongst the world's leading freight carriers and certainly in the forefront on the North Atlantic routes, despite the generally high tariffs that slowed the development of the air cargo industry.
Nevertheless, the airline introduced DC-8 freighters during the 1960s which paved the way for the arrival of the initial batch of Boeing 747s. The first seven examples of the latter were configured for passenger work, but in 1975 KLM received two of the new combi specimens.
This variant was offered by Boeing as a means to meet the growing demand for freight capacity, but at the same time handle a relatively smaller number of passengers. The Dutch flag carrier opted for a 208-seat layout which also enabled 12 containers to be carried in the rear main-deck cabin which was equipped with a large door for loading purposes. Of course, if necessary the aircraft could revert to a passenger-only mode capable of accommodating 408. KLM went on to become the world's largest operator of the 747 combi model, two of which were subsequently converted into dedicated freighters in the late 1990s.
The introduction of 10 Airbus A310s in the 1980s enabled the airline to carry freight in the underfloor holds using containers that were compatible with those of the 747s.
With schedules arranged to offer regular

connections at Schiphol for onward intercontinental flights, KLM's long-standing faith in the air cargo business proved to be justified.

Fleet:

Regn	Srs	C/n
Boeing 747		
PH-BFC	406 (SCD)	23982
PH-BFD	406 (SCD)	24001
PH-BFE	406 (SCD)	24201
PH-BFF	406 (SCD)	24202
PH-BFH	406 (SCD)	24518
PH-BFI	406 (SCD)	25086
PH-BFM	406 (SCD)	26373
PH-BFO	406 (SCD)	25413
PH-BFP	406 (SCD)	26374
PH-BFR	406 (SCD)	27202
PH-BFS	406 (SCD)	28195
PH-BFT	406 (SCD)	28459
PH-BFU	406 (SCD)	28196
PH-BFV	406 (SCD)	28460
PH-BUH	206B (F) (SCD)	21110
PH-BUI	206B (F) (SCD)	21111
PH-BUK	206B (SCD)	21549
PH-BUL	206B (SCD)	21550
PH-BUM	206B (SCD)	21659
PH-BUN	206B (SCD)	21660
PH-BUT	206B (SCD)	22380

KLM Cargo also contracts regular freight services to other carriers such as Schreiner Airways.

Korean Air Cargo (KE/KAL)

Head Office: 351 Konh Hang Dong, Kang Seo Ku, Seoul, South Korea
Tel: (2) 656 78 05 Fax: (2) 656 78 70

The company was created by the South Korean Government as Korean National Airlines in 1948, remaining so until 1962 when Korean Air Lines was formed. In March 1969 the carrier moved into the private sector when it was sold to the Hanjin Transport Group, the present owner. From 1973 the airline began to assemble a modern fleet which included Boeing 747s, this type being employed on international links with the US, while the route network was also expanded into Europe with Paris the first destination to be served. Korean was Airbus Industrie's first customer outside Europe when it ordered the A300 in September 1974, a relationship that has continued in the 1990s with the Series 600 and the A330. Finding a need for a type to supplement the 747s, Korean also ordered three DC-10-30s which were duly delivered in the spring of 1975. Two other machines were subsequently acquired although one of the fleet was lost in an accident at Anchorage in December 1983 and another while landing at Tripoli in 1989. Subsequently the type was used mainly for services in the Far East until the survivors were withdrawn in 1996.

In the meantime an extensive freight division was also established by Korean Air, the name adopted in 1984, building up a large fleet of Boeing 747s and a pair of Airbus A300s. In addition the airline became a launch customer for the MD-11 in 1986, although after delivery in 1991/2 three of the five were converted for dedicated cargo work. Destinations served include Basle, Brussels, Colombo, Delhi, Dubai, Johorubaru, Madras, Milan, Penang, Portland and Shenzhen.

In the late 1990s Korean Air suffered the loss of a number of aircraft, one of the freighter MD-11s being destroyed in April 1999. The poor safety record raised much concern amongst the authorities and threatened the carrier's career.

Fleet:

Regn	Srs	C/n
Airbus A300		
HL7278	F4-203	277
HL7279	F4-203	292
Boeing 747		
HL7403	4B5F (SCD)	26408
HL7405	2B5F (SCD)	24195

Regn	Srs	C/n	Regn	Srs	C/n
HL7408	2B5F (SCD)	24196	HL7470	3B5 (SCD)	24194
HL7424	2S4F (SCD)	22169	HL7471	273C (SCD)	20652
HL7441	230F	20373	HL7474	2S4F (SCD)	22169
HL7451	2B5F (SCD)	22480	HL7476	2B5F (SCD)	24196
HL7452	2B5F (SCD)	22481	HL7497	4B5F (SCD)	26401
HL7454	2B5F (SCD)	22482			
HL7458	2B5F (SCD)	22485	**McD Douglas MD-11**		
HL7459	2B5F (SCD)	22486	HL7372	AF	48408
HL7462	4B5F	26406	HL7374	AF	48410

L'Aéropostale (ARP)

Head Office: BP 10454, F-95708 Roissy-CDG, France
Tel: (1) 48 62 80 56 Fax: (1) 48 62 67 27

During 1987 Inter Cargo Service was formed in France, although it quickly became known as ICS Inter Ciel Service. In 1990 the latter revived the title L'Aéropostale when the opportunity came to take over the French domestic mail work. It was planned to use Boeing 737-300s for the night work but equipped with a Quick-Change (QC) facility to permit daytime operations with passengers.

The airline received its first aircraft suitably modified with a large cargo door and QC capability, the first such conversion carried out on the type. As the fleet expanded, so L'Aéropostale developed its domestic network of routes until it became the largest cargo carrier in the country, most of it moved at night.

Fleet:

Regn	Srs	C/n	Regn	Srs	C/n
Airbus A300			F-GIXA	2K2C	20836
F-GOZA	B4-102F	148	F-GIXB	33A(QC)	24789
F-GOZB	B4-102F	184	F-GIXC	38B(QC)	25124
F-GOZC	B4-102F	189	F-GIXD	33A(QC)	25744
Boeing 727			F-GIXE	3B3(QC)	26850
F-GKDY	225F	22438	F-GIXF	3B3(QC)	26851
F-GKDZ	225F	22441	F-GIXG	382(QC)	24364
Boeing 737			F-GIXH	3S3(QC)	23788
			F-GIXI	348(QC)	23809
F-GFUE	3B3(QC)	24387	F-GIXJ	3Y0(QC)	23685
F-BFUF	3B3(QC)	24388	F-GIXK	33A(QC)	24028
F-GFVI	230C	20256	F-GIXL	348(QC)	23810
F-GGVP	2K2C	20943	F-GIXO	3Q8(QC)	24132
F-GGVQ	2K2C	20944	F-GIXP	3M8(QC)	24021

Linea Aérea Nacional de Chile (LAN Chile Cargo) (LA/LAN)

Head Office: Estado 10, Piso 21, Casilla 147-D, Santiago de Chile, Chile
Tel: (2) 694 77 77 Fax: (2) 601 91 15

When formed by the government in 1929 the airline was known as Linea Aeropostal Santiago-Arica, taking its present name in 1932. Most of its early activities involved mail flights, but through the years scheduled passenger services were undertaken to neighbouring South American destinations, and as more modern equipment was introduced long-haul routes were added to the network. In fact LAN Chile was the first company to operate a twin-engined airliner across the South Atlantic when a Boeing 767-200 flew

the inaugural sortie with a revenue-earning service in 1986.
Privatised in 1990, the airline has since increased its involvement in freight working and now has a comprehensive route network serving domestic, North, Central and South America, Asia/Far East and Europe, the latter destinations being Amsterdam, Frankfurt, London, Madrid and Paris. In recent years the airline has carried out a short programme of flights to Stansted in the Christmas period carrying consignments of Chilean grapes for the UK market.

Fleet:

Regn	*Srs*	*C/n*	*Regn*	*Srs*	*C/n*
			Douglas DC-8		
Boeing 737			CC-CDS	71F	45996
CC-CEI	248C	20219	CC-CDU	71F	45997
Boeing 767			CC-CYQ	71F	45810
CC-CZZ	316F	25756	N872SJ	71F	46040

Lufthansa Cargo (LH/GEC)

Head Office: Postfach 1244, D-65441 Kelsterbach, Germany
Tel: (69) 696 5437 Fax: (69) 696 6886

Lufthansa Cargo became a wholly owned subsidiary of the German flag carrier in January 1995 in order to take over the worldwide freight business. This prompted a spate of restructuring within the company which resulted in a merger with German Cargo Services, another Lufthansa subsidiary. Originally formed in 1977, the airline initially operated two Boeing 707s, but another pair joined the fleet two years later mainly for the movement of split charters around the world.

A growing need for some increased capacity brought five Douglas DC-8-73s into the fleet at the expense of the pioneers, the newcomers offering a more efficient operation. In the early 1990s Lufthansa decided to integrate its own Boeing 747 freight operations with those of its subsidiary, at the same time creating Lufthansa Cargo Airlines. In addition, two Boeing 737-200s were employed for some years for feeder services, each aircraft

Above: Boeing 747 D-ABZF was built as a dedicated freighter and is operated by Lufthansa Cargo. *AJW*

being capable of carrying standard pallets and containers for onward transportation by the long-haul fleet. In 1995 Lufthansa Cargo ordered five (later increased to eight) MD-11Fs, the first two of which were delivered in July 1998. The aircraft were configured to carry 15,530cu ft of containerised cargo with a further 5,566cu ft available in the lower compartments. The enlarged hatch and semi-automatic loading system make it possible to achieve exceptionally fast turnarounds of less than 2.5 hours. In addition to the MD-11s that were due for delivery by the end of 1999, the airline holds options on another three. Although the type requires 25% less fuel per ton/kilometre than the 747, nevertheless Lufthansa Cargo plans to keep its 11 Boeing Srs 200s in service and considers the trijet as a supplement rather than a replacement. However, future plans may mark the gradual phasing out of the Boeing fleet.

Fleet (Cargo):

Regn	*Srs*	*C/n*	*Regn*	*Srs*	*C/n*
Boeing 747			**McD Douglas MD-11F**		
D-ABYO	230F (SCD)	21592	D-ALCA	AF	48781
D-ABYT	230BF (SCD)	22363	D-ALCB	AF	48782
D-ABYU	230F (SCD)	22668	D-ALCC	AF	48783
D-ABYY	230BF (SCD)	22671	D-ALCD	AF	48784
D-ABYZ	230BF (SCD)	23286	D-ALCE	AF	48785
D-ABZA	230BF (SCD)	23287	D-ALCF	AF	48798
D-ABZB	230F (SCD)	23348	D-ALCG	AF	48799
D-ABZC	230BF (SCD)	23393	D-ALCH	AF	48800
D-ABZF	230F (SCD)	23621	D-ALCI	AF	48801
D-ABZI	230F (SCD)	24138	D-ALCJ	AF	48802
			D-ALCK	AF	48803

Lynden Air Cargo (L2/LYC)

Head Office: 6441 South Airpark Place, Anchorage, AK 99502-1809, USA
Tel: (907) 243 0215 Fax: (907) 245 0213

Affiliated with Lynden Air Freight, the airline was formed in 1995 with operations commencing on 31 August. The carrier specialises in the transportation of oversized cargo worldwide using four of former Safair, South Africa, Lockheed Hercules for the purpose. Since the type is capable of landing on gravel, ice or short airstrips it is ideally suited to the inhospitable terrain to be found in Alaska. Regular scheduled services are also operated within the State to link Anchorage and Fairbanks with many locations that have difficult surface access. In addition the aircraft will land when required almost anywhere to pick up or unload its cargo. The company can also respond quickly to an environmental emergency such as an oil spill with dispersant spraying operations.
While the Hercules are employed on such emergency operations, the airline also has two Electras that are used for the more

Fleet:

Regn	*Srs*	*C/n*	*Regn*	*Srs*	*C/n*
Lockheed L-188 Electra			N402LC	30	4698
N281F	AF	1079	N403LC	30	4590
N289F	CF	1110	N404LC	30	4763
Lockheed L-100 Hercules					
N401LC	30	4606			

orthodox loads. The duo were bought from the Zantop collection and are still giving excellent service despite being almost 40 years old.

Malaysia Cargo (MH/MAS)

Head Office:33rd Floor, Bangunan MAS, Jalan Sultan Ismail, Kuala Lumpur, Federal Territory 50250, Malaysia
Tel: (3) 265 5434 Fax: (3) 263 3178

When formed by Straits Steamship, Ocean Steamship and Imperial Airways the airline was identified as Malayan Airways. This was changed to Malaysian Airways in 1963 to reflect the similar change of title for the newly renamed country. Three years later the governments of Singapore and Malaysia acquired joint control of the airline which was once again renamed, this time to Malaysia-Singapore Airlines in 1967. By the early 1970s it was felt that some restructuring was in order, which naturally resulted in the airline being divided into Singapore Airlines and Malaysian Airlines System, later further modified to Malaysia Airlines.
Subsequently the carrier expanded its fleet with modern wide-bodied types with World Airways providing some of the equipment. In fact the MD-11 freighter operated by MAS Cargo is leased from the US carrier for regular services to Europe where Frankfurt has been the centre of operations. Due to difficulties in expanding at the busy airport, on 28 March 1999 Malaysia relocated to the former US base at Hahn, a subsidiary of Frankfurt since 1998. Previously making two visits a week to the German destination, following the move MAS was able to double the frequency with two Boeing 747 and two MD-11 flights per week, increasing to daily as soon as possible. Cargo flights around the Malaysian region are handled by a pair of Boeing 737 freighters.

Fleet:

Regn	*Srs*	*C/n*
Boeing 737		
9M-MZA	3H6F	27125
9M-MZB	3H6F	27347
Boeing 747		
9M-MHI	236BF (SCD)	22304
9M-MHJ	236BF (SCD)	22442
9M-MHK	3H6 (SCD)	23600
9M-MHL	4H6 (SCD)	24315
9M-MHM	4H6 (SCD)	24405
McD Douglas MD-11		
N276WA	CF	48632

Martinair (MP/MPH)

Head Office: PO Box 7507, NL-1118 ZG Schiphol, Netherlands
Tel: (20) 601 12 22 Fax: (20) 601 13 03

Known originally as Martins Air Charter, the airline was formed in 1958 equipped with one DC-3 for ad hoc charters and pleasure flying. The takeover of the Rotterdam-based Fairways in 1964 marked the start of some steady expansion, which received significant assistance when KLM took a 25% share in the company which adopted the title Martinair Holland in 1968. This name remained unchanged until 1995 when 'Holland' was dropped.
The association with the Dutch flag carrier resulted in the latter transferring a number of aircraft to its subsidiary. Martinair introduced a convertible Douglas DC-10-30 in the mid-1970s, later becoming the operator of the first Airbus A310 (PH-MCB) to be produced with a large cargo door in the forward fuselage. The company's developing all-cargo operations resulted in the launch of a daily flight from Schiphol to the Far East with transit stops in the Gulf States. By this time a pair of Boeing 747 convertibles had been acquired for these duties, followed in the early 1990s by a dedicated 747 freighter acquired from Air France. Martinair also replaced its DC-10s with the MD-11, four examples of which were convertibles while two were delivered

in freighter configuration. The company also handles short and long-term leases for other major carriers in need of additional capacity. For instance, in March 1999 Martinair began a series of weekday flights between Brussels and Dayton, Ohio, using a freighter MD-11 (PH-MCU or MCW) for a US airline. On this occasion the contract covered some eight weeks of work and is typical of the type of business carried out by Martinair. The Dutch company finalised an agreement with Kenya Airways in May 1999 to operate joint freight flights in regional Africa, in this case by leasing an Antonov An-12.

Above: Martinair uses its MD-11s for cargo work, PH-MCT being a combi variant. *AJW*

Fleet:

Regn	*Srs*	*C/n*
Boeing 747		
PH-MCE	21AC (SCD)	23652
PH-MCF	21AC (SCD)	24134
PH-MCN	228F (SCD)	25266
McD Douglas MD-11		
PH-MCP	CF	48616
PH-MCR	CF	48617
PH-MCS	CF	48618
PH-MCT	CF	48629
PH-MCU	AF	48757
PH-MCW	AF	48788

The airline also operates six Boeing 767-31AERs for passenger work.

Martinaire (MRA)

Head Office: 8030 Aviation Place, Suite 2000, Dallas, TX 75235, USA
Tel: (972) 358 5858 Fax: (972) 350 7979

Martinaire is an overnight air freight support and on-demand air charter company located at Dallas, Texas, with its corporate offices, operations unit and maintenance facilities based at Dallas Love Field. The company operates over 30 scheduled routes for UPS, DHL and Airborne Express to all parts of the US using a fleet of Cessna 208 Caravans, Dornier 228s and Fairchild Swearingen Metros.

The carrier's maintenance division is equipped to work on most small to medium sized aircraft and is an accredited Cessna facility with its own avionics and parts department

Fleet:

Regn	Srs	C/n
Cessna 208 Caravan 1		
N1031P	208B	0404
N1115M	0356	0356
N1116W	208B	0411
N1117G	208B	0370
N4591B	208B	0137
N4602B	208B	0140
N4625B	208B	0159
N4655B	208B	0160
N4662B	208B	0161
N4674B	208B	0165
N4687B	208B	0167
N9331B	208B	0055
N9339B	208B	0057
N9448B	208B	0121
N9469B	208B	0079
N9471B	208B	0081
N9505B	208B	0085
N9529G	208B	0091
N9546B	208B	0126
N9594B	208B	0131
N9623B	208B	0138
N9714B	208B	0153
N9738B	208B	0097
N9760B	208B	0102

Regn	Srs	C/n
N9761B	208B	0107
N9762B	208B	0109
N9766B	208B	0112
N9956B	208B	0119
Dornier 228		
N110DN	203F	8110
N228ME	201	8097
N260MC	202	8121
N264MC	202	8144
N265MC	202	8149
N269MC	202	8135
N279MC	202	8120
Fairchild Metro II		
N515SS	SA226TC	TC-211

Regn	Srs	C/n
Fairchild Metro III		
N354AE	SA227AC	AC-633
N360AE	SA227AC	AC-675
N367AE	SA227AC	AC-691
N575MA	SA227AC	AC-756
N585MA	SA227AC	AC-684
N672AV	SA227AC	AC-672
N2693C	SA227AC	AC-659B

MK Airlines (7G/MKA)

Head Office: Landhurst, Hartfield, East Sussex TN7 4DL
Tel: (01892) 770 011 Fax: (01892) 770 022

The airline was founded in November 1990 by combining MK Airlines Ghana and Flash Airlines, with operations beginning during 1991 with a DC-8 freighter acquired from Connie Kalitta. Initially the aircraft was employed for cargo services between Africa and a variety of European airports in partnership with Cargo d'Or. However, MK was soon established as a leading freight carrier, with regular visits made to the UK using Stansted as the destination for much of the traffic until April 1999. At this point the airline announced that it was moving its once or twice-daily flights to Manston (Kent International), an airport which is steadily developing into a busy cargo terminal.

The reason for the change of gateway resulted from several infringements of the noise regulations, for which the company was fined a total of £1,000. While the DC-8s are undoubtedly noisy, at least the frequency of the movements is not great, unlike the Boeing 737-200s of Ryanair which are also generous with the distribution of decibels in far greater numbers. MK is also under contract to handle the air freight business between Belgium and Iceland where subsidiary MK Flugfelag was established in 1997.

Above: MK Airlines operates regular freight services from Africa to the UK using DC-8s such as 9G-MKF. Until May 1999 Stansted was the UK terminal, but following noise complaints the DC-8s now often stop at Manston in Kent. *AJW*

Fleet:

Regn	*Srs*	*C/n*	*Regn*	*Srs*	*C/n*
Douglas DC-8			TF-MKG	62F	46027
9G-MKA	55F	45804	TF-MKH	62F	46153
9G-MKC	55F	45692	**Boeing 747**		
9G-MKE	55F	45753	9G-MKI	245F	–
9G-MKF	55F	45820			

MK Flugfelag (MKI)

Head Office: Sudurlandsbraut 32, IS-128 Reykjavik, Iceland
Tel: (577) 32 00 Fax: (577) 32 02

See MK Airlines

MNG Cargo Airlines (MB/MNG)

Head Office: Yesikoy Caddesi 9, TR-34810 Florya-Istanbul, Turkey
Tel: (212) 663 83 52 Fax: (212) 573 35 30

This Turkish cargo carrier was formed in 1997 with operations commencing on 15 August. It flies scheduled freight services to a number of Middle and Far East destinations, together with regular visits to the UK at Stansted, Germany (Frankfurt) and Brussels. The company's first transatlantic sortie came in September 1998 followed by a scheduled flight to the US on 8 November. A once-weekly full freighter service is now offered from Istanbul to Montreal, the aircraft staging through Brussels. This routeing reduces flying times overall, producing the benefit of savings on fuel and additional payload capacity.

Above: Another airline that has started freight services with A300s is MNG Airlines from Turkey. Appropriately registered TC-MNG, the aircraft was originally with Hapag-Lloyd as D-AHLB in the early 1980s and was converted for cargo work at that time to become the first Series C4-203. *AJW*

Fleet:

Regn	*Srs*	*C/n*	*Regn*	*Srs*	*C/n*
Airbus A300			TC-	B4-203F	-
TC-MNA	B4-203F	019			
TC-MNG	C4-203	083			

Murray Aviation (MU/MUA)

Head Office: 835 Willow Run Airport, Ypsilanti, Michigan 48198-0899, USA
Tel: (913) 484 4800 Fax: (913) 484 4875

The carrier was formed in 1985 with operations commencing in December 1986. From the outset it was intended to offer on-demand cargo charters to both domestic and international destinations. The airline chose the CASA 212 for its operations, a type that can carry a maximum load of 6,000lb (2,722kg). Freight can be loaded into the 24ft cargo area via the rear ramp by using the roller system for the pallets or containers. The Spanish-built type also has an excellent short runway performance which allows the machine to use more remote airstrips that are often nearer to the final destination. This useful capability therefore reduces the amount of road transport required.

Nevertheless, the company also has a need for a small freighter, so a number of suitable types were therefore evaluated until eventually the Jetstream 31 was selected. An 11-year-old former US Airways Express specimen was acquired in March 1999, with work soon commencing on the conversion programme at the airline's base. Essentially the changes involve the removal of the passenger fittings and the installation of a strengthened floor, together with a large rear cargo door in the port side of the fuselage. A pressure bulkhead is provided aft of the flightdeck, which will also gain an escape hatch for the use of the crew when the cargo compartment is full. In the latter circumstances it will also serve as the entry door for the pilots.

After the modified Jetstream has gained its supplemental type certificate in early 2000, Murray intends to employ the aircraft for its own services. However, the company envisages that it will have a future need for up to 20 machines and also hopes to attract customers from North America, Europe and Australia.

Fleet:

Regn	Srs	C/n
CASA 212		
N262MA	200	262
N263MA	200	263
N287MA	200	287
N349TA	200	349
N687MA	200	174
BAe Jetstream		
N	3101	695

Nightexpress (EXT)

Head Office: Building 511, Room 3056, Frankfurt Airport, D-60549 Frankfurt, Germany
Tel: (69) 69 04 57 51 Fax: (69) 69 02 21 01

This German carrier was established in June 1984 with operations starting in the same month. The company has subsequently linked its home base with the UK, using Luton as the UK gateway for the six-times-weekly flights. The airline has attracted a number of regular customers for its services, although Nightexpress also offers ad hoc charters throughout Europe.

Fleet:

Regn	Srs	C/n
Beech 99		
D-IEXB	-	U-70
Short SD3-60		
D-CCAS	300	SH3737

Nippon Cargo Airlines (KZ/NCA)

Head Office: 10F Shin-Kasumigaseki Building, 3-2 Kasumigaseki 3 Chome, Chiyoda, Tokyo 100, Japan
Tel: (3) 35 07 41 00 Fax: (3) 35 07 41 69

When Nippon Cargo Airlines was formed in September 1978 it was Japan's first all-cargo carrier. A somewhat lengthy period then followed while the airline's application for an operating certificate received the attention of the authorities. Eventually this was received by NCA in August 1983, but a further two years passed before an inaugural service was flown to North America. Asian destinations were added during the following year, followed by Europe in 1988 using Amsterdam and Milan as gateways. London was served from December 1998, when a twice-weekly flight from Tokyo to Stansted was launched. NCA's Boeing 747s were all delivered new to the airline by the manufacturer with the exception of JA8158 that was built as a short-range variant for the Japanese market, and JA8192 which was previously with Royal Jordanian, British Caledonian and British Airways. It was converted to freighter configuration in 1997.

Below: Nippon Cargo Airlines often employs the Boeing 747-281F JA8191 for its twice-weekly Tokyo-Stansted scheduled service. *AJW*

Fleet:

Regn	Srs	C/n	Regn	Srs	C/n
Boeing 747			JA8188	281F (SCD)	23919
JA8158	SR-81F (SCD)	22711	JA8191	281F (SCD)	24576
JA8167	281F (SCD)	23138	JA8192	2D3F (SCD)	22579
JA8168	281F (SCD)	23139	JA8194	281F (SCD)	25171
JA8172	281F (SCD)	23350			

Northern Air Cargo (NC/NAC)

Head Office: 3900 West International Airport Road, Anchorage, AK 99502-1097, USA
Tel: (907) 243 3331 Fax: (907) 249 5193

Northern Air Cargo was formed in 1956 to become Alaska's first and only all-cargo airline, quickly establishing freight services utilising a pair of Fairchild C-82 Packets. This type proved invaluable when carrying outsized loads such as generators and vehicles to remote sites. The aircraft also delivered freight to rural communities and settlements on a charter basis, while emergency situations requiring specialised equipment such as after the Good Friday earthquake in 1964 confirmed the C-82's usefulness.

However, eventually the aircraft were retired in favour of the Douglas DC-6 and its former USAF C-118 counterpart until a total of 13 were on strength in 1999. Two of the aircraft are equipped with the useful swing-tail modification which was incorporated into one of them when it was serving with the now defunct Spanish carrier Spantax in the 1960s. The second was the responsibility of Kar Air, a subsidiary of Finnair. The feature allows large items to be loaded more easily and has proved to be a worthy successor to the C-82s. Each DC-6 can carry nearly 30,000lb (13,600kg) and they have operated NAC's scheduled cargo services to some 20 destinations for many years. However, the airline has introduced Boeing 727s to the fleet, which not only have a capacity of 48,000lb (21,770kg), but are equipped with hush-kits and gravel-kits to allow them to operate from noise sensitive airports and gravel runways.

Fleet:

Regn	Srs	C/n	Regn	Srs	C/n
Boeing 727			N1036F	C118A	43581
N190AJ	46F	18878	N1377K	C118A	44596
N930FT	23F	19387	N2907F	C118A	44636
N992AJ	23F	19428	N4206L	C118B	43709
			N4213X	C118A	44605
Douglas DC-6			N7919C	B	43554
N434TA	BF(ST)	44434	N7780B	A	45372
N779TA	AC	45529	N43872	C118A	44665
N867TA	BF(ST)	45202	N99330	C118A	43576
N1027N	C118A	43580	(ST = swing-tail)		

Northwest Cargo (NW/NWA)

Head Office: 5101 Northwest Drive, St Paul, Minnesota 55111-3034, USA
Tel: (612) 726 2111 Fax: (612) 726 6599

Originally known as Northwest Airways when it was formed in 1926, it followed the trend of the period by flying mail across the US. Passenger services were operated alongside this 'bread and butter' activity, but in 1934 the mail contracts ended. Presumably it had been agreed at the outset that in such an event the airline would be obliged to change its name, so in order to comply the carrier selected Northwest Airlines as its new identity, which at least demanded the minimum of effort by the signwriters.

It was changed once again in 1947 when the first polar flight from Seattle to Tokyo and Manila was introduced with DC-4s. On this occasion it was thought that the two new destinations warranted recognition in the company's name to emphasise the importance of the routes to the Far East. The airline therefore added Orient to its name, which then remained unaltered for the next 40 years or so. During this period Northwest had taken delivery of an impressive fleet of Boeing 707s in the early 1960s, some being equipped with side cargo doors. These were followed by five Boeing 747s early in the wide-bodied age, all configured as pure freighters.

In the mid-1980s Northwest merged with Republic, in the process acquiring a large number of domestic routes and a fleet of aircraft suitable for such operations. With most of the airline's growth now coming from within the US, Orient seemed less appropriate than hitherto, so it was decided to revert to Northwest Airlines with the freight division known as Northwest Cargo. The latter still employs dedicated Boeing 747 freighters, some of which have been with the company since new in the mid-1970s.

Fleet:

Regn	*Srs*	*C/n*	*Regn*	*Srs*	*C/n*
Boeing 747			N619US	251F (SCD)	21321
N616US	251F (SCD)	21120	N629US	251F (SCD)	22388
N617US	251F (SCD)	21121	N630US	2J9F (SCD)	21668
N618US	251F (SCD)	21122	N9401	249F (SCD)	22245

Polar Air Cargo (PO/PAC)

Head Office: 100, Ocean Gate, 15th Floor, Long Beach, CA 90802, USA
Tel: (562) 436 7471 Fax: (562) 436 9333

The airline was formed in 1993 by a partnership known as NedMark, Polaris Aircraft Leasing, which supplied the two aircraft for the launch and Southern Air Transport. It had been realised that the takeover of Flying Tigers by Federal Express could reduce the amount of capacity available for bulk loads, since the latter's main aim was to acquire the operating rights across the Pacific. Polar's first two aircraft were a pair of Boeing 747-100s that had been converted for cargo work after the collapse of Pan Am, their previous operator. The inaugural commercial sortie took place on 25 April 1993 and was a charter between New York and Vienna. This was followed a month later by the introduction of a scheduled freight service linking New York, Shannon and Moscow in association with Aeroflot. In due course this was extended to Hong Kong and onward to the US, the first transpacific venture flown by the airline. Expansion came quickly with the introduction of services to Sydney, Melbourne, Taipei and Prestwick which meant that the fleet of 747s was also increased until nine examples were on strength at the end of the first year of operations.

At this point the airline was certified as a supplemental carrier by the US Federal Aviation Administration (FAA), while the Department of Transportation issued a similar certificate recognising Polar as an all-cargo operator. Finally, in May 1995 the company became a US flag carrier, at the same time acquiring another three 747s to cover the addition of new destinations that included Buenos Aires, Santiago and Singapore. In the following year Amsterdam and London were added to the network together with the Brazilian cities of Manaus, São Paulo and Rio de Janeiro. Once again the fleet grew in sympathy to reach 14 examples of the 747, but the airline suffered a setback when the FAA issued a directive that restricted the payload for 747s converted by GATX-Airlog. Three of Polar's aircraft were affected by the action which effectively grounded the trio. Despite this loss of capacity, Polar remained loyal to the Boeing type, although the DC-10, MD-11 and TriStar were evaluated. The airline is now ranked as the number one all-cargo carrier in the US and the fourth largest in the world. The airline expanded its coverage on 2 December 1998 when it launched a twice-weekly scheduled freighter service to Tokyo/Narita. The initial sortie was flown over a Manila-Tokyo-Anchorage-Chicago-New York routeing and gave every indication of proving popular with the freight forwarders at each stop. Polar intended to increase the frequency during 1999 but this step was dependent upon the slot situation at Narita. The airline's latest venture followed closely behind with scheduled operations to Saudi Arabia and Africa, all part of the overall plan to meet the international air freight demand on a global basis.

Fleet:

Regn	*Srs*	*C/n*
Boeing 747		
N806FT	249F (SCD)	21827
N830FT	121F (SCD)	19642
N831FT	121F (SCD)	19648
N832FT	121F (SCD)	20347
N850FT	122F (SCD)	19755
N851FT	122F (SCD)	19756
N852FT	122F (SCD)	19757
N853FT	122F (SCD)	19753
N854FT	122F (SCD)	19754
N855FT	124F (SCD)	19733
N856FT	132F (SCD)	19897
N857FT	132F (SCD)	20246
N858FT	123F (SCD)	20109
N859FT	123F (SCD)	20326
N888KH	249F (SCD)	21827
N920FT	249F (SCD)	22237
N921FT	283F (SCD)	21575

Reliant Airlines (RLT)

Head Office: Willow Run Airport, PO Box 827, Ypsilanti, MI 48198-0899, USA
Tel: (734) 483 3616 Fax: (734) 483 2629

In the early 1980s the founder of Reliant Airlines considered that the Dassault Falcon 20 was an ideal aircraft for the proposed on-demand charter work envisaged for the future company. The type had earlier been responsible for the rapid growth of Federal Express, so when the latter decided to withdraw all of its cargo-door-equipped Falcon 20s in 1983, it was an opportunity to convert Reliant from a paper airline into reality.

The new company was founded in April 1984 with the resolve to provide a service that did not exist in the industry. The company's first aircraft was Falcon 20 N226R which was purchased from Federal Express on 10 May 1984, with flight operations commencing during the next month. The type's suitability for the express package business had already been proven by FedEx, but strangely Reliant found itself the only carrier offering the cargo-door Falcon despite its large capacity for freight and its ability to offer a rapid response time for urgent shipments.

At this early stage there were only three employees, but growth came quickly and by 1987 the airline had become the largest operator of the modified Falcons with a fleet that now comprised six specimens. A useful customer base had also been established amongst both the motor industry and the express package market which had developed a healthy demand for more participants.

The company's continued success came from the hard work that produced a unique service upon which the customers could depend. In 1996 the founder, Reese Zantop, sold a majority shareholding to the employees, which in turn generated an even greater sense of interest in the well-being of the company's affairs.

By 1998 the airline's fleet had grown to 13 Falcon 20s for freight work together with one Falcon 10 passenger-configured aircraft used to support customer personnel movements. During the year Reliant also purchased a DC-9-15F dedicated freighter and applied to the Government for operating authority. In due course this was received and a second example joined the fleet, the larger machines being earmarked for ad hoc charters and for scheduled routes flown for the customers.

Fleet:

Regn	Srs	C/n	Regn	Srs	C/n
Dassault Falcon			N230RA	20D	230
N8GA	10	127	N301R	20D	3
N108R	20D	108	N560RA	20C	56
N126R	20D	126	N810RA	20C	81
N192R	20D	192	N950RA	20C	95
N212R	20D	212	N980R	20C	98
N226R	20D	226			
N227R	20D	227	**Douglas DC-9**		
N229R	20D	229	N410AM	15F (RC)	47010
			N568PC	15F	47086

Royal Nepal Airlines

(RA/RNA)

Head Office: PO Box 401, RNAC Building, Kantipath, Kathmandu, 711000 Nepal
Tel: (1) 220757 Fax: (1) 225348

Formed by the Government in 1958, Royal Nepal became responsible for all the domestic and international routes between Nepal and India. The airline serves some 37 destinations from Kathmandu, with the more lengthy flights handled by a pair of Boeing 757s, the first example joining the company in 1987. A second machine was delivered during the following year, this time configured for combi working. Capable of carrying three containers in the forward section of the fuselage, up to 148 passengers can also be accommodated in the rear cabin. When delivered in September 1988, Royal Nepal had the distinction of operating the first such variant to enter service. Subsequently the 757 has enabled Royal Nepal to provide both industry and tourists with easy access to the country, including a twice-weekly visit to Gatwick via Frankfurt.

Fleet:

Regn	Srs	C/n	Regn	Srs	C/n
Boeing 757			9N-ACB	2F8C	23863
9N-ACA	2F8	23850			

Ryan International Airlines

(HS/RYN)

Head Office: 6810 West Kellogg, Wichita, Kansas 67209-2218, USA
Tel: (316) 942 0141 Fax: (316) 942 7949

Formed in 1972 as Ryan Aviation, the airline started operations during the following year as a subcontractor to Emery Express using seven Cessna Citations. The company was acquired by the PHH Group in 1985, but four years later the founder, Ronald Ryan, managed to repurchase the organisation. Equipped with DC-9s and Boeing 727s, the airline began regular mail flights on behalf of the US Postal Service, once again as a subcontractor to Emery. Each aircraft begins its nocturnal activities at an outstation city, carrying its load to the Indianapolis hub where the consignment is sorted. The machine then returns to its home base for express and priority mail delivery in that particular area.

A similar system is used by Emery for its overnight air freight activities, although in this case the superhub is located at Dayton, Ohio, which is visited nightly by the outstationed aircraft. From the start of Emery's express operations 20 years or so ago, Ryan has always managed a good proportion of the aircraft and has continued to achieve a level of reliability in its performance that is the envy of the industry generally.

This employment therefore provides much of Ryan International's income and indeed most of the aircraft carry the liveries of its customers. However, during

Above: Ryan International leases the Boeing 727-22C N428EX from Emery although it flies under contract to the US Postal Service carrying the latter's full livery and titles. *K. Buchanan via G. Pennick*

the summer of 1995, the airline began operations for the National Fisheries Corporation, a Federated States of Micronesia organisation flying out of Guam in the South Pacific. Fresh tuna is airlifted daily from the islands such as Palau, Pohnpei, Truk and Yap and taken to Guam for subsequent transportation to the Japanese sushi and sashimi markets.

Fleet:

Regn	Srs	C/n	Regn	Srs	C/n
Boeing 727			N428EX	22C	19097
N94GS	44F	18892	N429EX	22C	19100
N210NE	31F	18903	N432EX	151C	19867
N220NE	31F	18905	N433EX	151C	19868
N329QS	21F	19038	N435EX	51C	19288
N355QS	21F	19257	N436EX	51C	19289
N356QS	21F	19258	N526PC	77C	20370
N357QS	21F	19259	N527PC	172C	19665
N359QS	21F	19007	N528PC	82C	19597
N413EX	51C	19206	N721JE	76F	18843
N414EX	51C	18899	N753AS	22C	19203
N416EX	51C	19287	N8892Z	225F	21861
N417EX	51C	19290	N17789	232F	20643
N421EX	22C	19099			
N426EX	22C	19089	**Douglas DC-9**		
N427EX	22C	19090	N568PC	15F	47086

SAS Cargo (SK/SAS)

Head Office: Fack, S-195 87 Stockholm-Bromma, Sweden
Tel: (8) 797 00 00 Fax: (8) 85 79 80

This division of the airline now plays a leading role in the movement of freight to and from Scandinavia which covers all of Denmark, Norway and Sweden, most of Finland and the Baltic area. A high proportion of this traffic is carried on intra-European scheduled passenger flights which provide the high frequencies demanded by customers. In the case of the Boeing 767s and 747s pallets and containers are used, but the rest of the fleet carry bulk-loaded items. North America represents a high growth area and is expected to triple in volume during the next 20 years or so. SAS already operates 50 transatlantic sorties per week including the last daily departure from Copenhagen at 19.30. This still allows shipments to arrive in New York on the same day with the option of onward travel to one of over 70 destinations.

Until early 1999 dedicated cargo services were operated between Gothenburg, Sharjah and Macau using Boeing 747-200F N523MC on lease from Atlas Air. When this was terminated SAS replaced it with a Gothenburg-Sharjah-Hong Kong link, but this time contracting Lufthansa Cargo to supply an MD-11F for the duty.

Fleet:
Aircraft on scheduled passenger services used with long-haul operations covered by leased equipment.

Schreiner Airways (AW/SCH)

Head Office: PO Box 381, NL-2130 Hoofddorp, Netherlands
Tel: (23) 555 55 55 Fax: (23) 555 55 00

Since it was formed in 1945, Schreiner has been involved in most aspects of the air transport industry. Such activities include helicopter and fixed-wing operations in support of the oil companies in the North Sea area in co-operation with KLM. During the past few years the carrier has acquired a fleet of Dash Eights which have been used for scheduled passenger services on behalf of Sabena. Recently the company acquired the first of three Airbus A300 freighters, whereupon KLM contracted the company to operate its weekly freight flights between Schiphol, Milan/Malpensa and Bologna, thereby replacing HeavyLift on these runs.

Sabena is also reorganising its franchise agreement with Schreiner to remarket the services as Sabena Connect. The latter employs four Dash Eights for the duties but the total number of aircraft and routes is likely to increase after September 1999. The Canadian machines were also due to be joined by a pair of ex-Air Nostrum ATR72s in August.

Fleet:

Regn	*Srs*	*C/n*	*Regn*	*Srs*	*C/n*
Airbus A300			PH-SFL	B4-203F	220
PH-SFK	B4-203F	211	PH-SFM	B4-203F	274

Simba Air Cargo (SMB)

Head Office: PO Box 59224, Nairobi, Kenya
Tel: (2) 53 35 25 Fax: (2) 53 35 29

This privately owned company started operations in 1995 by flying perishable freight from Kenya to the European markets. One Boeing 707 was acquired for the duties which involved the aircraft visiting Amsterdam three times weekly. Subsequently the company has added Brussels, Kigali, Mombasa and Ostend to its coverage which is still the responsibility of the original and now ageing 707. For the first 10 years of its career it served the British national carrier as G-AYLT, but since 1981 it has been operated by a variety of airlines, the majority being African.

Fleet:

Regn	*Srs*	*C/n*
Boeing 707		
5Y-SIM	336C	20517

Singapore Airlines (SQ/SIA)

Head Office: Airline House, 25 Airline Road, Singapore 819829
Tel: (65) 542 33 33 Fax: (65) 545 50 34

In the immediate postwar years Malayan Airways was formed to provide commercial services that linked Singapore, Kuala Lumpur, Ipoh and Penang. The flights were operated by several Airspeed Consuls, the civil conversion of the military twin-engined Oxford. Steady traffic growth was soon experienced, so by 1955 an impressive fleet of DC-3s was employed to maintain the scheduled services throughout the region. Later the carrier experienced several renaming processes which included the adoption of the title Malaysian Airways in 1963, followed three years later by a change to Malaysian-Singapore Airlines (MSA) after the two governments had gained joint control. This time the airline survived for several years without further amendments to its identity, but on 1 October 1972 MSA ceased operations in favour of Malaysian Airline System (later Malaysia Airlines) and Singapore Airlines. The latter already possessed a comprehensive route network covering much of South-East Asia, so it now began to expand the intercontinental routes. A start was made in 1968 with the purchase of three Boeing 707s followed by the first Boeing 747s in 1973. Through the years a profitable and popular carrier, in 1989 the arrival of the Boeing 747-400 enabled nonstop flights to be introduced to London. In the same year SIA's first dedicated 747-200 freighters entered service, although these pioneers were subsequently replaced with eight Series 400Fs known to the company as 'Mega Arks'. Claimed to be the most advanced commercial cargo aircraft in the world, the variant has a range of 5,123 miles (8,245km) carrying a full payload of 117 tonnes.

The volume of cargo carried by the aircraft justified the construction of a facility to handle the goods. Officially known as Cargo Terminal 5, the SIA superhub was built at Singapore Changi Airport in 1995 and is capable of handling over 450,000 tonnes of cargo within its 28,000sq m confines. Three elevating transport vehicles are used within the terminal, each able to move fully-laden containers of up to 6,800kg quickly and efficiently. Nevertheless, the constant growth of the business has meant that a second terminal is planned to be operational in 2001. SIA 6 will be located alongside its partner and will boost the handling capacity at the hub by 750,000 tonnes.

Singapore is not alone in needing such facilities because SIA operates a recently-opened warehouse at San Francisco which is capable of handling 50,000 tonnes of cargo. A similar unit designed to handle 90,000 tonnes was due for completion at Los Angeles in mid-1999, effectively doubling the current capacity.

Fleet:

Regn	*Srs*	*C/n*	*Regn*	*Srs*	*C/n*
Boeing 747			9V-SFE	412F (SCD)	28263
9V-SFA	412F (SCD)	26563	9V-SFF	412F (SCD)	28026
9V-SFB	412F (SCD)	26561	9V-SFG	412F (SCD)	26558
9V-SFC	412F (SCD)	26560	9V-SKM	312 (SCD)	23409
9V-SFD	412F (SCD)	26553	9V-SKP	312 (SCD)	23769

Below: Singapore Airlines operates a number of Boeing 747-412 dedicated freighters which the airline has named 'Mega Arks'. In this case 9V-SFF was carrying Formula One racing cars. *AJW*

South African Airways Cargo (SA/SAA)

Head Office: PO Box 7778, Johannesburg 2000, South Africa
Tel: (11) 978 11 27 Fax: (11) 978 11 26

Union Airways was a private South African company founded in August 1929 to provide regular services between Cape Town, Durban, Johannesburg and Port Elizabeth. However, its main purpose was to ensure the swift movement of mail between these points, initially carried by DH Gipsy Moths of limited capacity. The airline's independence was not of a long duration, since in February 1934 it was acquired by South Africa Airways, itself newly-formed by the Government as a subsidiary of South Africa Railways.

Throughout the 1930s the airline developed an extensive network of routes within Africa, but it was in 1945 that a service was inaugurated to London using leased Avro Yorks. The journey was something of an endurance test, so travellers were relieved when the type was replaced by DC-4s and later Constellations. The introduction of the Comet was a significant advance for the airline in 1953, but was destined to be short-lived due to the tragic crashes of the type. After another spell with the piston-engined DC-7 replacement, SAA re-entered the jet age with three Boeing 707s. There were further problems for the carrier since, due to the political situation in the country, sanctions were imposed by neighbouring nations that prevented overflying their territory. It was necessary to reroute the European services and employ long-range types such as the Boeing 747 and later 767ERs.

With the lifting of the restrictions in 1993, SAA was able to expand its operations. The company had been an early customer of Airbus Industrie, one of the aircraft acquired being the first A300C4 combi to come off the assembly line at Toulouse in 1982. After delivery SAA used it for passenger work, but with the rapid growth of the cargo industry, the machine became a dedicated freighter employed mainly for regular services to Europe. By the mid-1990s it was apparent that there was sufficient demand for more capacity, so in 1995 it was decided to convert one of the passenger-configured Boeing 747-200s. The machine involved had joined the company in 1980, but after 15 years or so began its new career by linking Johannesburg and Durban with Frankfurt twice weekly, together with regular sorties to New York. A pair of Boeing 737s were similarly converted for use on regional cargo operations in Africa, while Southern Air Transport became the source for an additional 747 freighter in 1998.

Below: Boeing 747 ZS-SAR is employed as a freighter by South African Airways. *A. S. Wright*

Fleet (Cargo):

Regn	Srs	C/n	Regn	Srs	C/n
Airbus A300			ZS-SIF	244F	22585
ZS-SDG	C4-203	212	**Boeing 747**		
Boeing 737			ZS-SAR	244B (SCD)	22170
ZS-SID	244F	22583	ZS-SBJ	212F (SCD)	24177

Southern Air

Head Office: Columbus, Ohio
Tel: n/a Fax: n/a

Southern Air was formed in mid-1999 to replace Southern Air Transport (SAT) which ceased operations on 25 September 1998. The new airline applied to the US Department of Transport to take over the failed carrier's route authority and a number of its assets, with the intention of starting commercial flying in September. The airline plans to employ a fleet of up to five Boeing 747-200 freighters, the first specimen having been acquired from Lufthansa Cargo Airlines in June.

Fleet:

Regn	Srs	C/n
Boeing 747		
N	230BF (SCD)	22669

Star Air (SRR)

Head Office: Copenhagen Airport South, DK 2791, Dragoer, Denmark
Tel: 32 31 43 43 Fax: 32 31 43 90

Operations began in 1984 for this new carrier which began charter work with a number of Fokker Friendships. Now wholly-owned by the A. P. Moller Group, also the parent of Maersk Air, Star Air concentrates its activities on the operation of scheduled freight services on behalf of UPS. By the mid-1990s the airline had disposed of its turboprop fleet in favour of Boeing 727s.

Fleet:

Regn	Srs	C/n	Regn	Srs	C/n
Boeing 727			OY-UPM	31C	19229
OY-UPA	31C	19233	OY-UPS	31C	19232
OY-UPD	22C	19103	OY-UPT	22C	19094
OY-UPJ	22C	19102			

Sterling European Airlines (NB/SNB)

Head Office: Copenhagen Airport, DK 2791, Dragoer, Denmark
Tel: 42 35 35 35 Fax: 32 45 13 91

The company was established in 1994 following the demise of its predecessor Sterling Airways, a leading Danish carrier that had been operating charters since 1962. Sterling European has subsequently resumed such activities, but in addition it is also contracted to operate TNT's fleet of Boeing 727 freighters.

Fleet (Cargo):

Regn	Srs	C/n	Regn	Srs	C/n
Boeing 727			OY-SEU	243F	21269
OY-SER	232F	20639	OY-SEV	281F	20571
OY-SES	251F	19977	OY-SEW	287F	21688
OY-SET	227F	21245	OY-SEY	224F	20659

Tampa Colombia (Transportes Aereos Mercantiles Panamericanos) (QT/TPA)

Head Office: Carrera 76 No 34A-61, Apartado Aereo 494, Medellin, (Antioquia), Colombia
Tel: (4) 250 29 39 Fax: (4) 250 56 39

Operations began in 1974, a year or so after the airline was launched. Initially one DC-6 was employed for freight flights in South America, but with the addition of a second specimen in 1975, Miami was added to the list of destinations served by the carrier. The purpose of the visits was to ferry freshly-cut flowers from Colombia, which in turn helped to establish a market for perishable produce in the country. During 1980 the airline acquired a pair of Boeing 707s for the freight links with the Florida airport, but after a year one machine was returned to the lessor and the second crashed in December 1983.

Undeterred, during the next few years five 707s joined the company, partly as a result of some expansion into Europe, using Ostend, Belgium, as the gateway. This sortie was normally covered by one of three DC-8s which were also taken on strength in the late 1980s/early 1990s. Eventually the 707s were withdrawn from the transatlantic missions to be replaced on a temporary basis by a DC-10-30 leased from World Airways.

Fleet:

Regn	*Srs*	*C/n*
Boeing 707		
HK-3333X	321C	18714
HK-3604X	324C	19352
Douglas DC-8		
HK-3785X	71AF	46066
HK-3786X	71AF	45849
HK-4176X	71AF	45945

Titan Airways (T4/AWC)

Head Office: Enterprise House, Stansted Airport, Stansted, Essex CM24 1QW, England
Tel: (1279) 680616 Fax: (1279) 680110

The company was launched in January 1988 with a single Cessna 404. This was used for both passenger charters and mail work for the Post Office, an activity that has subsequently been developed. Titan operates ad hoc charters throughout the

Above: Registered G-ZAPK, the aircraft is one of three BAe 146s employed by Titan Airways for either contract or ad hoc charter work. *AJW*

UK, mainland Europe, North Africa and the Middle East employing ATR-42s and BAe 146s for this business. The nightly movement of mail is carried out over the routes linking Leeds/Bradford with Stansted and Norwich with East Midlands and Liverpool. The airline also operates scheduled passenger services on behalf of other carriers short of capacity. Titan was due to add a Boeing 737-300 to its fleet in May 1999 with the first flight scheduled for 8 June. While the machine is available for general charter work, there is no intention to operate it in a freighter configuration.

Above: Titan Airways uses Aérospatiale ATR-42 G-BUPS for both passenger and freight duties.
G. W. Pennick

Fleet:

Regn	*Srs*	*C/n*
Aérospatiale ATR-42		
G-BUPS	300	109
G-ZAPJ	312	113
BAe 146		
G-ZAPK	200QC	E2148
G-ZAPL	200	E2030
G-ZAPN	200QC	E2119
Short SD3-60		
G-ZAPD	300	SH3741

TMA of Lebanon (TL/TMA)

Head Office: Beirut International Airport, PO Box 11/3018 Beirut, Lebanon
Tel: 961 (1) 629 210 Fax: 961 (1) 629 219

Trans Mediterranean Airways was formed in 1953 with operations starting during the same year using a pair of Avro Yorks for non-scheduled cargo flights. Later in the decade the airline received approval to offer scheduled services with two DC-4s initially, but gradually the fleet grew until by the early 1960s seven examples of the piston-engined type were on strength. More modern equipment was introduced in 1966 when TMA took delivery of its first Boeing 707 freighter, which was subsequently used for worldwide cargo services. Meanwhile the jet fleet steadily expanded until it contained nine examples by the mid-1970s. There was a noteworthy event in 1975 when the carrier acquired its first Boeing 747. The former American Airlines machine promptly began a regular service between its home base in the Lebanon, Amsterdam, London and New

York. Unfortunately the arrival of a second 747 in 1976 came at a time when Beirut was becoming distinctly unhealthy due to a civil war in the area. With the situation deteriorating, Beirut Airport was closed for over a year during which time TMA suspended operations until the situation improved. In all five 707s were destroyed during the period but the sale of the 747s prevented them from becoming the objects for target practice. Nowadays TMA operates scheduled cargo services to a wide variety of destinations in the Middle and Far East and Europe still equipped with the venerable 707, albeit in reduced numbers. Nevertheless, the time is approaching for the type's retirement, an event that will become necessary by 2001. The airline began seeking finance to fund the purchase of new equipment during 1999, but no details of the proposed replacement were forthcoming. However, it was reported that the Airbus A300 freighter is the most likely to take over the duties from the 707s.

Fleet:

Regn	*Srs*	*C/n*	*Regn*	*Srs*	*C/n*
Boeing 707			OD-AGS	331C	19214
OD-AGD	323C	18939	OD-AGX	327C	19104
OD-AGO	321C	19269	OD-AGY	327C	19105
OD-AGP	321C	19274			

TNT Express Worldwide (NTR)

Head Office: Stead House, 2-6 Frances Road, Windsor, Berks SL4 3AA
Tel: (01753) 84 21 68 Fax: (01753) 85 81 58

Today, aircraft displaying the colours of the freight carrier TNT are a familiar sight at many of Europe's airports yet the airline had its origins in Australia in 1946 when it was formed as Thomas Nationwide Transport. The carrier subsequently played a significant role in the development of the freight industry before becoming a public company in 1961. After considering a number of options for expansion, in 1978 it was decided to enter the European market, duly accomplished by acquiring a number of existing organisations. With these transactions completed, the company went on to add the IPEC Courier Group's European division and the freight carrier SkyPak to its possessions in 1983. It resulted in TNT becoming increasingly active throughout the UK and near Continent, although at this stage all movements were handled by a road transport network.

While the system had worked well, the growth of the industry meant that a faster and more efficient service was needed. The solution came in 1987 when TNT announced that it proposed to set up an air network with dedicated freighters. The type chosen for the role was the BAe 146-200QT (Quiet Trader) for which TNT became the launch customer. This variant had a cargo door installed in the port side of the rear fuselage together with an integrated roller floor to facilitate the essential fast turn-rounds. Before the regular airlift could be launched a major problem had to be overcome. As an Australian company, TNT could not function as an airline, particularly over the routes planned, due to the strictly observed traffic rights. It was therefore necessary to contract the flying to carriers that possessed the necessary authority. After inviting applications from four airlines, Luton-based Air Foyle was eventually chosen. This company already had some experience of such work, having been the first to operate an overnight courier service between the UK and mainland Europe in 1979.

Following the delivery of the first BAe 146, its inaugural sortie for TNT was made on 5 May 1987 between Prestwick and Nuremburg, the airport chosen as the hub for the operations. There were some doubts raised within the industry about the company's decision to invest so heavily in new equipment instead of using elderly, converted passenger aircraft that were far cheaper and readily available. However, TNT intended to offer a very reliable service from the outset and this was not considered possible with 30-year-old types. In addition the 146 would not be affected by the forthcoming noise restrictions and indeed had attracted a 10% reduction in landing fees at some airports.

There was immediate satisfaction with the 146QT's performance, a fact soon confirmed when TNT announced an order for 72 examples. The majority of these were intended for the European network, but others were to be allocated for leasing or resale. In the event the order proved somewhat optimistic; although the fleet did expand, the total number of 146s was well short of the ambitious target. Financial restraints were partially responsible for the change of policy, but the rapid growth experienced tended to outgrow the capacity of the 146 which meant that a larger type would be needed in the not too distant future.

In the meantime the small carrier XP Parcels was absorbed, but even more significantly TNT moved its central European hub to more spacious and conveniently located accommodation at Cologne/Bonn. The steady increase in traffic by the various courier companies was not appreciated by the local population around the German airport, which received a constant stream of complaints. In addition the facilities at Cologne were already proving too small, thereby creating unwanted congestion and delays. After some four years spent evaluating various sites TNT selected the former Belgian military airfield at Liège for its new hub. Construction at the site began in November 1996, continuing steadily until the company was able to transfer its nocturnal activities in March 1998.

As expected earlier, the demand for TNT's services began to exceed the carrier's capacity, so it was decided to introduce hush-kitted Boeing 727s flown by Hunting Cargo. It was not long before the type's 23-tonnes payload was proving invaluable and resulted in a further five examples of the trijet entering service, although the Danish airline Sterling European later took over the operation of the type. Despite meeting the Stage III noise regulations, it is unlikely that the 727s will continue beyond 2002. Even a hush-kitted specimen can still generate more than its fair share of decibels when departing with 23 tonnes of cargo.

Above: One BAe 146 (G-TJPM) has been operated by TNT in the livery and titles of Sky Pak, one of the companies acquired by the worldwide express operator. *AJW*

Above: Most of TNT's loads are containerised and are easily stowed via the 146's large loading door. *TNT*

Studies into suitable replacements short-listed the Airbus A300 which offers a payload of 39 tonnes and the 29-tonnes capacity Boeing 757. Eventually the A300 freighter conversion was chosen, the first of its kind to appear in TNT livery during 1998 being G-CEXI on lease from Channel Express pending delivery of up to 14 examples of the wide-bodied type.

However, in May 1999 the company embarked on some major restructuring involving the setting up of its own freight

Above: TNT also has aircraft operating in the Far East on similar duties to those in Europe. The 146 G-TNTD has now returned to the UK but is still wearing its Pacific East Asia Cargo titles it acquired in 1993. However, it has exchanged its RP-C481 identity for the original British registration. *AJW*

Fleet:

Regn	Srs	C/n
Airbus A300B4		
G-BYDH	203F	210
G-CEXI	203F	121
(leased from Channel Express)		
G-	203F	227
G-	203F	247
G-	203F	-
BAe 146		
D-	200QT	E2109
D-	200QT	E2112
EC-ELT	200QT	E2102
EC-EPA	200QT	E2089
EC-FFY	300QT	E3154
EC-FVY	200QT	E2117
EC-FZE	200QT	E2105
EC-GQO	200QT	E2086
EC-GQP	200QT	E2100
EC-	200QT	E2056
G-TJPM	300QT	E3150
G-TNTB	200QT	E2067
G-TNTE	300QT	E3153
G-TNTG	300QT	E3182
G-TNTK	300QT	E3186
G-TNTL	300QT	E3168
G-TNTM	300QT	E3166
G-TNTR	300QT	E3151
I-TNTC	200QT	E2078
Boeing 727		
OY-SER	232F	20639
OY-SES	251F	19927
OY-SET	227F	21245
OY-SEU	243F	21269
OY-SEV	281F	20571
OY-SEW	287F	21688
OY-SEY	224F	20659
OY-TNT	281F	20725

Below: TNT's latest colour scheme is carried by the Airbus A300 G-CEXI, a machine leased from Channel Express. *AJW*

airline to be headquartered at Liège. After gaining its air operator's certificate by the end of the year, TNT intends to commence operations with the first of its ordered A300s. This will end the contract with Air Foyle, although it is expected that the latter's pilots will be invited to transfer to the new airline since some of the 146s will remain in service. Sterling will continue to operate the 727 fleet which should be replaced by the A300s by 2001.

Tol-Air Services (TI/TOL)

Head Office: PO Box 37670, Airport Station, San Juan, PR 00937-0670, USA
Tel: (787) 791 5235 Fax: (787) 791 8385

Founded in 1983 by Jorge A. Toledo, Tol-Air began its cargo and passenger services on 16 May using a Cessna 182 for regular links with Borinquen and Beef Island. This aircraft was soon joined by a Beech 18 configured as a dedicated freighter for scheduled flights to St Maarten, St Eustatius and St Kitts.

During 1988 the airline acquired three

DC-3s, from which point the number of aircraft on strength and the route network steadily grew, until in 1992 the first turboprop type was added to the fleet. This was a Metro II and was intended to maintain the cargo link between San Juan and the Dominican Republic. Nowadays Tol-Air is the largest air cargo and charter operator in the Caribbean region, flying to 10 destinations daily carrying up to 100,000lb (45,360kg) of freight. Puerto Rico is now linked with St Thomas, St Croix, St Maarten, Tortola, Martinique, Guadeloupe and St Kitts, while the main cargo facilities are located at Munoz Marin Airport in San Juan.

Fleet:

Regn	*Srs*	*C/n*
Beech 18		
N28V	E18S	BA-130
N52A	E18S	BA-114
N353T	G18S	BA-485
N398B	E18S	BA-329
N779T	H18	BA-618
Convair 240		
N147JR	T29C	403
N357T	T29C	340
Douglas DC-3C		
N780T	C47B	20865
N781T	R4D1	4306
N782T	C47	4382
N784T	C47	6054

Tradewinds Airlines (WI/TDX)

Head Office: 7304 West Market Street, Greensboro, North Carolina 27409, USA
Tel: (910) 668 7500 Fax: (910) 668 7517

The company has operated under several names through the years starting with Blue Bell Aviation in 1969. It later became a subsidiary of the Wrangler Corporation, thereupon adopting Wrangler Aviation as its new identity. The airline was equipped with four Canadair CL-44s which were employed for general cargo services throughout the USA on behalf of its parent company. In November 1991 the carrier's name was changed once more, this time to become Tradewinds International Airlines, although 'international' was later dropped from the title, by which time it had expanded its fleet with the help of a TriStar.

There was a setback in July 1993 when the US authorities gave the company four months in which to restructure its affairs This followed the discovery that it was majority owned or controlled by interests from Singapore. A review of the situation was carried out in August which proved to be satisfactory after some managerial changes had been implemented to ensure that the airline was a US organisation.

In 1997 the carrier decided to widen its coverage with the operation of passenger charter flights. Approval was duly received to fly domestic and international services with a fleet of up to five aircraft, allowing the first trip between Boston and Montego Bay to be made on 15 February 1998. These sorties were undertaken by additional TriStars, but after a year or so the carrier decided to end its involvement in passenger work to revert to its original status of a dedicated cargo operator. Five TriStar 200s and two Series 1s were therefore returned to the lessor, leaving the airline with one Series 1 configured as a freighter.

Fleet:

Regn	*Srs*	*C/n*
Lockheed L-1011 TriStar		
N311EA	1F	1012

Transafrik International (STH)

Head Office: Sao Tomé International Airport, Sao Tomé, Sao Tomé e Principe
Tel: (2) 39 33 97 Fax: (2) 35 41 62

This charter airline provides contract cargo and passenger services together with large scale medical evacuation flights when necessary. The company specialises in the movement of outsized items of cargo into difficult locations that are otherwise inaccessible. Formed in 1984, the carrier operates mainly within Africa.

Fleet:

Regn	*Srs*	*C/n*	*Regn*	*Srs*	*C/n*
Boeing 727			**Lockheed L-100 Hercules**		
S9-CAA	95F	19836	S9-CAI	30	4562
S9-CAB	23F	19182	S9-CAJ	30	4565
S9-CAH	22F	18849	S9-CAV	30	4301
S9-NAZ	82F	19404	S9-CAW	30	4300
S9-TAO	23F	19390	S9-CAX	30	4248
			S9-CAY	30	4208

Trans Arabian Air Transport (TO/TRT)

Head Office: PO Box 1461, 69 Africa Street, Khartoum, Sudan
Tel: (11) 45 15 68 Fax: (11) 45 15 44

This privately owned company was formed in 1983 for the purpose of offering cargo charter flights to destinations such as Addis Ababa, Amsterdam, Athens, Cairo, Doha, Harare, Jeddah, London, Malta, Nairobi, Port Sudan and Sharjah. The fledgling airline operated one DC-8 at the start of operations, but a second machine was acquired two years later. Both were replaced by two Boeing 707s in 1988/9, but one of these was lost in a crash during 1990, a leased example also suffering the same fate in the same year.

Despite these disasters, the cargo flights continued with the remaining machine until it was sold in the US. Several other 707s have had short stays with the airline, but rarely more than two at any one time. From the early 1990s Trans Arabian also leased three Antonov An-26s from Aeroflot, but these gradually dwindled in number until all had been returned by 1996.

Fleet:

Regn	*Srs*	*C/n*	*Regn*	*Srs*	*C/n*
Boeing 707			ST-APC	351C	19412
ST-AMF	321C	19367	5X-ARJ	351C	19632

Trans Continental Airlines (TCN)

Head Office: 803 Willow Run Airport, Ypsilanti, MI-48198, USA
Tel: (734) 484 3435 Fax: (734) 484 7144

The airline was originally formed in 1972 as International Airlines Academy following some reorganisation within the former Universal Airlines Training Centre. Nevertheless, it was 1975 before the carrier received its FAA Operator's Certificate that allowed it to fly for hire with cargo aircraft. Having achieved approval from the authorities, the company adopted a new identity in 1977, thereafter being known as Trans Continental Airlines (TCA) based at Willow Run, Detroit. It was inevitable that this location would bring a close association with the resident car manufacturers, with much of the airline's fleet involved in the movement of components between the various assembly plants. When launched the airline was equipped with eight ex-military Curtiss C-46s but these were steadily replaced by Convair 440s and a number of larger capacity DC-6s. By the 1980s TCA was also operating scheduled cargo services linking Chicago O'Hare with Minneapolis St Paul, Cleveland and Cincinnati in addition to its contract freight operations. During 1987 the airline acquired its first jet transport when an ex-United Airlines DC-8 was taken on strength, a type that has since remained the mainstay of the company.

Fleet:

Regn	*Srs*	*C/n*	*Regn*	*Srs*	*C/n*
Boeing 727			N184SK	61F	45981
N721SK	2B6F	21298	N185SK	54F	45679
N1186Z	21C	19134	N187SK	62AF	46022
N2688Z	44C	20476	N802BN	62F	45909
Douglas DC-8			N811TC	55F	45883
N181SK	62F	45910	N812TC	55F	45764
N182SK	55F	45817			
N183SK	62F	45904			

Turkish Cargo

Head Office: General Administration Building, Atatürk Airport, TR-34830 Istanbul, Turkey
Tel: (212) 663 63 00 Fax: (212) 663 47 44

Although Turkish Airlines is mainly involved in passenger services both scheduled and charter, the airline also has a cargo division which was formed in the early 1980s. It was initially equipped with a pair of Boeing 707s which were employed for much of the time to carry fruit and vegetables from Istanbul to Frankfurt in order to connect with transatlantic services. The duties were later taken over by three late production Boeing 727s that were converted for cargo work in the mid-1990s. Although the Turkish produce is also destined for the European markets, these consignments tend to be distributed through the relatively quiet southern Netherlands airport at Maastricht, while Stansted handles UK-bound goods.

Fleet:

Regn	*Srs*	*C/n*	*Regn*	*Srs*	*C/n*
Boeing 727			TC-JCB	2F2F	22993
TC-JCA	2F2F	22992	TC-JCD	2F2F	22998

Below: Turkish Airlines still has a few Boeing 727s left in its fleet, mostly for cargo work. One of the survivors involved in this pursuit is TC-JCB. *AJW*

United Airlines (UA/UAL)

Head Office: PO Box 66100, Chicago, IL 60666, USA
Tel: (847) 700 4000 Fax: (847) 700 7680

When formed in 1926 the airline was involved in mail flights across the US but has since built itself into the world's second largest airline in terms of revenue with a fleet of nearly 600 aircraft flying on a worldwide route network. In fact, United is the largest passenger and freight combination carrier in the US.
Until 1997 the airline used the cargo capabilities of its mainline fleet, the volume handled playing a large part in the company's success. With a growing need for more capacity, the airline began operating its DC-10s configured as freighters to supplement the belly loads carried by the passenger division. The trijets entered service on the Pacific routes, linking key cities in North America with Asian gateways at Tokyo, Osaka, Seoul, Taipei and Manila. It is the largest airline to operate over the Pacific and is also developing routes in South America. Elsewhere United has become one of the leading transatlantic operators with nonstop services to Europe, many of them flown by Boeing 777s which can carry impressive loads of freight. Nevertheless, the airline has recognised the value of the dedicated freighters and will undoubtedly increase the number operated.

Fleet (Cargo):

Regn	*Srs*	*C/n*
Douglas DC-10		
N1852U	30F	47811
N1853U	30F	47812
N1854U	30F	47813
N1855U	30F	47837
N1856U	30F	46975
N1857U	30F	46986
N1858U	30F	46987
N1859U	30F	47819

UPS-United Parcel Service (5X/UPS)

Head Office: 1400 North Hurstbourne Parkway, Louisville, KY 40223, USA
Tel: (502) 329 65 00 Fax: (502) 329 65 50

One of the major express carriers in the world, United Parcel Service (UPS) was founded at Seattle in 1907. Even as early as 1929 the company appreciated the value of air transport for the speedy movement of packages, so the use of passenger airliners began for this purpose. Unfortunately, the venture coincided with the Wall Street Crash which ended any plans for an overnight service. The company resumed its previous activities following this setback, remaining firmly on the ground until 1953 when a two-day UPS-AIR service was launched between major US cities. In 1982 it entered the overnight delivery market that had been created by Federal Express, initially offering the benefits of UPS Next Day Air, followed three years later by UPS International Air.

In order to carry out these operations, the company bought seven ex-Braniff Boeing 727s, at the same time establishing a hub at Louisville, Ky. UPS quickly became one of the fastest growing airlines in the world with Boeing 747s and Douglas DC-8s augmenting the growing number of 727s in the fleet. Unusually, the company did not operate any of its possessions, which nonetheless carried the owner's full livery and titles. Instead, the work was contracted out to other carriers such as Evergreen International, Interstate Airlines, Orion Air and Ryan International. This arrangement continued successfully until 1987, when UPS realised that it could achieve lower costs and greater flexibility with increased control, by taking over the operations.

Subsequently the airline has invested heavily to improve its efficiency in the highly competitive overnight delivery industry. An order for 20 Boeing 757PFs (Package Freighters) in 1985 resulted in the aircraft being developed to the company's specification, which included moving the crew-entry door forward to allow an additional container to be carried. The first example was delivered by Boeing in September 1987 and is now one of 70 of the type employed by UPS for its US domestic work.

More drastic action was necessary with the 59 Boeing 727s, since they did not meet the forthcoming Stage 3 noise regulations. It was therefore decided to replace the existing Pratt & Whitney JT8Ds with Rolls-Royce Tay 651 turbofans to produce a quiet, fuel-efficient and more reliable aircraft than the previous versions. In addition, the airline embarked upon a programme to refit the flightdecks with electronic instruments and modern avionics, thereby introducing some standardisation to the fleet. Now known as the 727QF (Quiet Freighter), the work was completed in December 1996, well ahead of the deadline for the implementation of Stage 3. It gave UPS the distinction of becoming the first major US carrier to achieve 100% compliance with the noise restrictions and therefore avoids the harsh penalties already imposed by some airports.

Understandably, those living in the vicinity of hubs such as Cologne are opposed to the growing number of night flights. In reality, none of the airlines chooses to fly at such times to take advantage of lower costs or because there is less congestion. The reason is purely to meet the wishes of the customers who constantly request later pick-ups and earlier deliveries, which inevitably results in the sorties being flown under the cover of darkness. Without them companies would be at a major disadvantage so overnight delivery remains a significant factor for the modern express industry. At least UPS operates the quietest freighters possible, a fact that was responsible for the carrier being granted an extension to its night flights into Cologne until 2015.

The regular transatlantic operations now mainly employ a growing fleet of Boeing 767-300ERs with stops at East Midlands, Stansted and Cologne. Although deliveries of the Boeing wide-body began in late 1995, negotiations with staff restricted its use to the domestic scene in the US. With problems resolved, the type has taken over the long-haul responsibilities with no particular machine dedicated to the duties. Its introduction has enabled UPS to lower the daily utilisation of the DC-8-73 fleet which it has no intention of retiring until around 2008.

An intra-European network is flown in support by some 40 aircraft mainly chartered from other carriers. However, UPS has a number of its own 727QFs based

Above: UPS uses Boeing 747 freighters for long-haul work, N683UP being a former FedEx machine. *A. S. Wright*

Above: Not a shot of London's Jubilee Line extension but the empty interior of a United Parcel Boeing 767-300. *AJW*

Above: The freighter version of the Boeing 767 has a large loading door in the port side of the forward fuselage. *AJW*

on the Continent, one of which acts as a standby for additional capacity when required. The routes link some dozen cities to the German hub and play their part in the continued growth of the international express business.

Unusually, in order to employ some of the US-based 727s at the normally quiet weekends, UPS decided to adapt several for passenger work in the seasonal peak periods. The aircraft were then operated on holiday flights to Florida and the Caribbean very successfully, with few adverse comments from the travellers about their mode of transport.

Above: Normal UPS colours are carried by N303UP *A. S. Wright*

Above: DC-8s were used for some years by UPS for its nightly transatlantic services to the UK and Germany, but these are now operated by the Boeing 767s. *AJW*

Fleet:

Regn	Srs	C/n
Boeing 727		
N207UP	247F (QF)	21699
N208UP	247F (QF)	21701
N209UP	247F (QF)	21698
N210UP	247F (QF)	21697
N211UP	247F (QF)	21700
N212UP	247F (QF)	21392
N213UP	2A1F (QF)	21341
N214UP	2A1F (QF)	21342
N902UP	51C (QF)	18898
N903UP	51C (QF)	18945
N904UP	51C (QF)	18946
N905UP	51C (QF)	18947
N906UP	30C (QF)	19314
N907UP	27C (QF)	19118
N908UP	27C (QF)	19114
N909UP	27C (QF)	19115
N910UP	27C (QF)	19117
N911UP	27C (QF)	19119
N912UP	62C (QF)	19244
N913UP	62C (QF)	19245
N914UP	27C (QF)	19246
N915UP	27C (QF)	19533
N916UP	172C (QF)	19808
N917UP	30C (QF)	19310
N918UP	30C (QF)	19008
N919UP	30C (QF)	19012
N920UP	180C (QF)	19873
N922UP	31C (QF)	19231
N924UP	31C (QF)	19234
N925UP	31C (QF)	19230
N928UP	22C (QF)	19091
N929UP	22C (QF)	19092
N930UP	22C (QF)	19096
N931UP	25C (QF)	19858
N932UP	25C (QF)	19856
N933UP	25C (QF)	19857
N934UP	21C (QF)	19135
N935UP	1A7C (QF)	20143
N936UP	108C (QF)	19503
N937UP	25C (QF)	19302
N938UP	173C (QF)	19506
N939UP	27C (QF)	19532
N940UP	185C (QF)	19826
N941UP	22C (QF)	19196
N942UP	22C (QF)	19101
N946UP	25C (QF)	19721
N947UP	25C (QF)	19722
N948UP	25C (QF)	19357
N949UP	25C (QF)	19717
N950UP	25C (QF)	19718
N951UP	25C (QF)	19850
N954UP	185C (QF)	19827
OY-UPA	31C (QF)	19233
OY-UPB	180C (QF)	19874
OY-UPD	22C (QF)	19103
OY-UPJ	22C (QF)	19102
OY-UPM	31C (QF)	19229
OY-UPS	31C (QF)	19232
OY-UPT	22C (QF)	19094

The OY-registered 727s operated by Star Air

Regn	Srs	C/n
Boeing 747		
N520UP	212F (SCD)	21943
N521UP	212F (SCD)	21944
N523UP	283F (SCD)	22381
N671UP	123F (SCD)	20323
N672UP	123F (SCD)	20324
N673UP	123F (SCD)	20325
N674UP	123F (SCD)	20100
N675UP	123F (SCD)	20390
N676UP	123F (SCD)	20101
N677UP	123F (SCD)	20391
N680UP	SR46F (SCD)	20923
N681UP	121F (SCD)	19661
N682UP	121F (SCD)	20349
N683UP	121F (SCD)	20353
N691UP	121F (SCD)	19641
Boeing 757		
N401UP	24APF	23723
N402UP	24APF	23724
N403UP	24APF	23725
N404UP	24APF	23726
N405UP	24APF	23727
N406UP	24APF	23728
N407UP	24APF	23729
N408UP	24APF	23730
N409UP	24APF	23731
N410UP	24APF	23732
N411UP	24APF	23851
N412UP	24APF	23852
N413UP	24APF	23853
N414UP	24APF	23854
N415UP	24APF	23855
N416UP	24APF	23903
N417UP	24APF	23904
N418UP	24APF	23905

Regn	Srs	C/n
N419UP	24APF	23906
N420UP	24APF	23907
N421UP	24APF	25281
N422UP	24APF	25324
N423UP	24APF	25325
N424UP	24APF	25369
N425UP	24APF	25370
N426UP	24APF	25457
N427UP	24APF	25458
N428UP	24APF	25459
N429UP	24APF	25460
N430UP	24APF	25461
N431UP	24APF	25462
N432UP	24APF	25463
N433UP	24APF	25464
N434UP	24APF	25465
N435UP	24APF	25466
N436UP	24APF	25467
N437UP	24APF	25468
N438UP	24APF	25469
N439UP	24APF	25470
N440UP	24APF	25471
N441UP	24APF	27386
N442UP	24APF	27387
N443UP	24APF	27388
N444UP	24APF	27389
N445UP	24APF	27390
N446UP	24APF	27735
N447UP	24APF	27736
N448UP	24APF	27737
N449UP	24APF	27738
N450UP	24APF	25472
N451UP	24APF	27739
N452UP	24APF	25473
N453UP	24APF	25474
N454UP	24APF	25475
N455UP	24APF	25476
N456UP	24APF	25477
N457UP	24APF	25478
N458UP	24APF	25479
N459UP	24APF	25480
N460UP	24APF	25481
N461UP	24APF	28265
N462UP	24APF	28266
N463UP	24APF	28267
N464UP	24APF	28268
N465UP	24APF	25482
N466UP	24APF	28269
N467UP	24APF	25483
N468UP	24APF	25484
N469UP	24APF	25485
N470UP	24APF	25486
N471UP	24APF	28842
N472UP	24APF	28843
N473UP	24APF	28846
N474UP	24APF	28844
N475UP	24APF	28845
N476UP	24APF	-
N477UP	24APF	-
N478UP	24APF	-
N479UP	24APF	-
N480UP	24APF	-

Boeing 767

Regn	Srs	C/n
N301UP	34AFER	27239
N302UP	34AFER	27240
N303UP	34AFER	27241
N304UP	34AFER	27242
N305UP	34AFER	27243
N306UP	34AFER	27759
N307UP	34AFER	27760
N308UP	34AFER	27761
N309UP	34AFER	27740
N310UP	34AFER	27762
N311UP	34AFER	27741
N312UP	34AFER	27763
N313UP	34AFER	27764
N314UP	34AFER	27742
N315UP	34AFER	27743
N316UP	34AFER	27744
N317UP	34AFER	27745
N318UP	34AFER	27746
N319UP	34AFER	27758
N320UP	34AFER	27747
N322UP	34AFER	27748
N324UP	34AFER	27750
N325UP	34AFER	27751
N326UP	34AFER	27752
N327UP	34AFER	27753
N328UP	34AFER	27754
N329UP	34AFER	27755
N330UP	34AFER	27756
N331UP	34AFER	27757

Douglas DC-8

Regn	Srs	C/n
N700UP	71F	45900
N701UP	71F	45938
N702UP	71F	45902
N703UP	71F	45939
N705UP	71F	45949

Regn	Srs	C/n	Regn	Srs	C/n
N706UP	71F	46056	N805UP	73F	46117
N707UP	71F	45907	N806UP	73F	46006
N708UP	71F	46048	N807UP	73F	46007
N709UP	71F	45914	N808UP	73F	46008
N713UP	71F	46014	N809UP	73F	46109
N715UP	71F	45915	N810UP	73F	46001
N718UP	71F	46018	N811UP	73F	46089
N729UP	71F	46029	N812UP	73F	46112
N730UP	71F	46030	N813UP	73F	46059
N744UP	71F	45944	N814UP	73F	46090
N748UP	71F	45948	N818UP	73F	46108
N750UP	71F	45950	N819UP	73F	46019
N752UP	71F	45952	N836UP	73F	45936
N755UP	71F	46055	N840UP	73F	46140
N772UP	71F	46072	N851UP	73F	46051
N779UP	71F	45979	N852UP	73F	46052
N797UP	71F	45897	N866UP	73F	45966
N798UP	71F	45898	N867UP	73F	45967
N801UP	73F	46101	N868UP	73F	45968
N802UP	73F	46100	N874UP	73F	46074
N803UP	73F	46073	N880UP	73F	46080
N804UP	73F	46004	N894UP	73F	46094

Above: In order to advertise its support of the Olympics, United Parcels painted its Boeing 767 N320UP in a special livery. *AJW*

VARIG (RG/VRG)

Head Office: 365 Avenue Almirante Silvio de Noronha, Edificio Varig, CEP-20021-010 Rio de Janeiro, Brazil
Tel: (21) 272 50 00 Fax: (21) 272 57 00

Viacao Aérea Rio-Grandense (VARIG) was formed in May 1927 by the Condor syndicate in Brazil which was a subsidiary of Lufthansa. The airline built up a large domestic network before World War 2, an event that forced Varig's German president to vacate his post. During this period the carrier introduced its first international services, but it was not until the end of hostilities in 1945 that any major expansion was attempted. The availability of cheap, surplus military transports such as the C-46 Commando and C-47 Dakota meant that the fleet could be rapidly increased in size, paving the way for Varig to become South America's largest airline.

Jet-powered equipment was introduced in 1959 when three Caravelles joined the company followed by a pair of Boeing 707s for the longer-range services. The latter grew in numbers considerably in 1965 when Varig was awarded the European services previously flown by Panair do Brazil. An order was placed with Douglas for 12 DC-10-30s in the early 1970s with service entry planned for 1974. In the meantime cargo services were handled by a number of Boeing 727s and 707s, but the latter were phased out in the 1980s after two of the carrier's DC-10s had been converted into freighter configuration. The company's cargo division now operates throughout the world with its three trijets and is likely to receive additional capacity from more of the type after conversion. This step became necessary because of the airline's severe financial situation after the devaluation of Brazil's currency in January 1999.

Fleet (Cargo):

Regn	*Srs*	*C/n*
Boeing 727		
PP-VLD	41F	20425
PP-VLE	172C	19666
PP-VLG	41F	20423
PP-VLS	173C	19508
PP-VLV	30C	19009
Douglas DC-10		
PP-VMQ	30F	46941
PP-VMT	30F	47841
PP-VMU	30F	47842

Volga-Dnepr Airlines (VI/VDA)

Head Office: Ulitsa Karbisheva 14, 432062 Ulyanovsk, Russia
Tel: (8422) 20 14 97 Fax: (8422) 20 26 75

The airline was formed in 1990 and took the names of two rivers in the region as its identity. It operated its first flight in October 1991 and has since specialised in the movement of outsize cargo. The company has a marketing agreement with UK-based HeavyLift Cargo Airlines to offer the 150-ton-payload Antonov An-124 to the industry for operations worldwide. One example is usually on standby at Stansted to meet any sudden requirement.

Fleet:

Regn	*Srs*	*C/n*
Antonov An-124		
RA-82042	100	9773054055093
RA-82043	100	9773054155101
RA-62044	100	9773054155109
RA-82045	100	9773052255113
RA-82046	100	9773052255117
RA-82047	100	9773053259121
RA-82078	100	9773054559153
Ilyushin IL-76		
RA-76401	TD	1023412399
RA-76758	TD	0073474203

WDL Aviation (WDL)

Head Office: Cologne/Bonn Airport, PO Box 980267, D-51130 Cologne, Germany
Tel: (2203) 96 70 Fax: (2203) 96 71 05

The carrier was formed in 1955 with its base at Essen-Mulheim. Its main business involved charters, but other occupations such as air survey, pleasure flights and aerial photography also played a part of the company's activities for many years. Until the mid-1970s the airline's fleet consisted of a motley collection of types suitable for the equally varied duties, but in 1974 WDL obtained the second prototype Fokker F27 which thereafter remained with the carrier until 1995. In the meantime it was joined from time to time by other examples of the type, although their arrival was spread over a number of years. Eventually WDL concentrated most of its operations on cargo work and by 1999 was mainly equipped with the F-27 Srs 600, a variant built with the advantages of a large freight door in the port side of the forward fuselage. This is particularly useful when handling express parcels on behalf of TNT and UPS.

Fleet:

Regn	*Srs*	*C/n*	*Regn*	*Srs*	*C/n*
Fokker F-27			D-AELH	400	10340
D-ADEP	600	10318	D-AELI	600	10514
D-ADOP	600	10316	D-AELJ	600	10342
D-AELC	600	10438	D-AELK	600	10361
D-AELD	600	10442	D-AELM	600	10450
D-AELE	600	10477	D-BAKB	600	10261
D-AELF	600	10323	D-ABKC	600	10195
D-AELG	400	10338	D-ABKD	600	10179

World Airways (WO/WOA)

Head Office: 13873 Park Centre Road, Suite 490, Herndon, VA-22071, USA
Tel: (540) 834 9200 Fax: (540) 834 9412

World was formed in March 1948 and was duly awarded its operating certificate as a supplemental carrier with worldwide operating authority. The company acquired a fleet of Boeing 314 flying boats which were employed for charter flights between New York and Puerto Rico. Unfortunately, although a very comfortable transport, it lacked the flexibility and speed of the modern landplanes that were emerging after the war. Consequently during 1949 the 314s were withdrawn and replaced with a pair of ex-military Curtiss C-46 Commandos. These comprised the fleet when the airline was bought in 1950 by Edward J. Daly for $50,000.

Under his control, the company started coast-to-coast charters and also provided passenger and freight operations in support of construction work within the Arctic Circle. During 1956 the airline acquired two Douglas DC-4s, a type that was to be the mainstay of the fleet until 1960. An effort was made to secure more Government contracts but they were not particularly plentiful at that time. Meanwhile the two DC-4s were kept active on ad hoc work until 1956 when World was one of the carriers contracted to fly refugee and relief flights during the Hungarian Revolution, eventually making 14 transatlantic sorties to Europe. When this political skirmish had ended, the airline continued its military employment by carrying personnel and stores on transcontinental routes. This was quickly followed by a succession of similar contracts that encouraged major expansion within the company. Therefore after operating a fleet of two aircraft at the beginning of 1960, World found itself with about 20 DC-6s, Super Constellations and Starliners by the summer of 1962.

Jet re-equipment began in 1963 when three Boeing 707s were delivered, one operating the first nonstop westbound commercial flight across the Pacific from Oakland to Tokyo on 10 August. Transatlantic charters soon followed, but when deliveries of six Boeing 727s began in 1967 they were used for military contract work in the Far East. World became an all-jet carrier in 1969 but delivery of the three Boeing 747s ordered in 1966 was postponed in favour of six DC-8s, although the wide-bodied type eventually joined the company in 1973.

The early 1970s were very profitable times for World. It played a major role in the US involvement in the Vietnam war, probably more than any other carrier. Support flights were constantly provided, while the airline was also responsible for the delivery of the Forces newspaper, Stars and Stripes, to Vietnam from Japan where it was printed. The US Government considered this to be an important task aimed at maintaining the morale of the troops fighting in an inhospitable area of the globe for reasons largely unknown.

As early as 1967, World had sought an opportunity to fly schedules but was always thwarted by Government objections. This obstacle was finally removed on 24 October 1978 when the Airline Deregulation Act was passed, thereby freeing the airline industry of many of the unpopular restrictions of the past. In anticipation of this development, the airline ordered an additional Boeing 747 together with six DC-10-30s. It was the latter type that inaugurated the Los Angeles-New York operation on 11 April 1979, but less than six weeks later the type was grounded by the FAA following the crash of an American Airlines machine at Chicago. It had an immediate effect on World's fortunes, which were not improved by a four-month strike by the aircrews.

When the labour disagreements had been settled, the company launched a transatlantic schedule from Baltimore to London and Frankfurt, but the heavy price discounting by the competition had a damaging effect on the airline's finances, resulting in a succession of annual losses of over $20 million each year. Obviously it was a situation that could not continue, but before any action could be taken, Edward Daly died at the age of 61. Without his leadership the company continued to flounder, recording more substantial losses in 1984 and 1985. At last, after a varied selection of Chief Executive Officers had failed to turn the airline round, T. Coleman Andrews, a former advisor to President Gerald Ford, became President and CEO. Under his direction it was planned that in future World would concentrate on its traditional business of military, cargo and contract flying for other airlines. Scheduled services that had produced the cumulative losses of over $200 million in the late 1980s were dropped, while the headquarters were moved from Oakland, its home for some 30 years, to Washington-Dulles. The opportunity was also taken to rationalise the fleet, so all the 727s and 747s were sold or returned to the lessors. This left the

Fleet:

Regn	*Srs*	*C/n*	*Regn*	*Srs*	*C/n*
Douglas DC-10			**McD Douglas MD-11**		
N107WA	30F	46836	N274WA	AF	48633
N117WA	30	48318	N275WA	CF	48631
9M-MAW	30	46959	N276WA	CF	48632
9M-MAV	30	48283	N277WA	ER	48743
9M-MAZ	30	46933	N278WA	ER	48746

Below: The MD-11 N271WA in a basic scheme but with World titles in readiness for a lease to another carrier. *K. Buchanan via G. Pennick*

DC-10 as the sole type on strength until the delivery of the MD-11s began in 1993. During the 1990s World has continued its contract flying for the cargo industry and the military. Wet-leasing has also proved profitable, accounting for more than 80% of the business activities in 1997.

Zantop International Airlines (VK/ZAN)

Head Office: Hangar Two, 840 Willow Run Airport, Ypsilanti, 48198-0840 Michigan, USA
Tel: (313) 485 89 00 Fax: (313) 485 48 13

Named after the family that formed the airline in 1972, Zantop International began by providing charter cargo services from the Detroit/Willow Run facility. Much of this was work that specialised in the movement of components between the local car factories and the subcontractors' production lines scattered around the US. However, the airline was able to expand its activities from 1978 when it received authorisation to fly general cargo sorties throughout the country.

Initially Zantop used a number of DC-6 freighters for its services. These were supported by examples of the Convair 340/440 range that were built in the early 1950s, but had been subsequently re-engined with turboprops to produce the Model 640. The type proved ideal for the duties especially since a large side cargo door was installed. Indeed many of the aircraft have survived and remain in store at Willow Run in 1999 while awaiting a buyer. Another former passenger airliner acquired in large numbers for cargo work in the late 1970s was the Lockheed Electra. Used for domestic freight charters, the type was also leased out by the airline, with several examples operated by Bournemouth UK-based Channel Express from time to time.

Zantop entered the jet age in 1978 when a DC-8-54F was acquired to enable the airline to undertake long-haul charters. The aircraft remained the only jet in the fleet until 1984 when the first of seven DC-8-62s arrived in order to expand the coverage, but in 1988 all were sold. Eventually two former United Airlines Srs 54s were introduced in 1991, remaining with the airline throughout the decade, albeit out of service.

Fleet:

Regn	*Srs*	*C/n*
Convair 640F		
N5509K	-	66
N5510K	-	76
N5511K	-	171
N5512K	-	134
N5515K	-	133
N7529U	-	58
Douglas DC-8		
N8041U	54F	45675
N8042U	54F	45676

Regn	*Srs*	*C/n*
Lockheed Electra		
N282F	L188AF	1084
N284F	L188AF	1104
N286F	L188AF	1146
N290F	L188CF	1133
N340HA	L188CF	1109
N341HA	L188PF	1035
N343HA	L188AF	1053
N344HA	L188AF	1038
N346HA	L188AF	1043
N5507	L188AF	1012
N5510L	L188AF	1014
N5512	L188AF	1017
N5517	L188AF	1023
N5522	L188AF	1033